PRAISE FOR
THE GRIEF GUIDEBOOK

The pain of grief and loss evokes tough questions. **The Grief Guidebook: Common Questions, Compassionate Answers, Practical Suggestions** tackles the mental fog, the emotional despair, the physical setbacks, and the spiritual needs common to grievers. Roe gives positive affirmations and practical tools to help the griever's journey. If you're asking questions and going through grief, get this **go-to** resource to help you get through.

– Dr. Charles W. Page, MD, author of A Spoonful of Courage for the Sick and Suffering

The most comprehensive book on grief I've read. The genius of this book is its ability to speak to anyone who is grieving, regardless of the situation. The book serves as a voice of compassionate authority that speaks a word of hope and healing because it was born in the smelter of personal pain and despair. The suggestions and grief skills are crucial because they serve as the tools that facilitate the integration of pain and healing, both integral to achieving new life. Well done!

Grief is often filled with confusion and a litany of unanswered questions. Where do you even start to find an answer? Gary has been involved with helping the bereaved for as long as I have known him. In his new book, **The Grief Guidebook**, Gary takes these years of experience and creates a simple, practical reference for all the questions that the bereaved or someone helping the bereaved has (and even some they don't yet know they have). The answers he shares meet the griever where they are on this complicated and challenging road with the compassion, gentleness, and expertise needed to help them find their direction on the journey of grief.

Gary Roe's new book on grief is exactly what I needed and wished I had seven years ago after my daughter passed away. I particularly love that each chapter has its own affirmation to use when you are stuck in that category. For example, when I am stuck on the "why" questions, such as "why" did this happen to me, there is a wonderful affirmation that speaks to that. There is a terrific chapter on changing relationships after loss and so much more. This is the club you never wanted to join, but at least Gary is there with you helping you make sense of it all.

– Annette Hines, Esquire,
Special Needs Law Firm of Massachusetts

Gary knows how to write for the grieving heart. His books have helped so many of my clients in their grief journey and I know this latest book **The Grief Guidebook: Common Questions, Compassionate Answers, Practical Suggestions** will be of great help to everyone as well. As a grief counselor, I have been asked these questions many times and know this book will be of great benefit to me, my clients, and everyone who is traveling on this journey.

– Joan Pruitt,
Licensed Professional Counselor,
Hospice of Wichita Falls

Having experienced, and still being on the grief journey following the passing of my husband from Young Onset Alzheimer's Disease, and having read many of Gary's other books, this book stands alone for those grieving the loss of a loved one. The empathetic and practical approach, which answers so many of the questions those grieving may have, re-enforces the importance of grieving well and step by step adjusting to a new way of life. Gary has a unique and special way of approaching grief that truly helps and supports the grieving soul.

> – **Sylvia Bryden-Stock,**
> **author, speaker, Master Coach**

To whom do you ask the difficult, pointed questions about your grief when it is all consuming? Gary Roe has walked this road in his own life and supported numerous others. Listening, learning, and loving others through his God-given compassion is a gift to grieving hearts everywhere. I will share this book with clients and friends in years to come.

> – **Carrie Andree Gardner,**
> **Licensed Professional Counselor**

I love this book. The question-and-answer format makes the information accessible and concrete. Once you identify your concern, you can find it in the table of contents and read about it. Rather than advice, Gary provides options. You can choose a possible solution that works with your personality. Chapters are easy to read, brief, and intensely practical.

> – **Debra Johnson, MDiv,**
> **Hospice Bereavement Coordinator**

When we are facing a personal loss, we all long for guidance and wish for an instruction book on what to do. This is the closest thing I have seen. It is a great resource for understanding the grief process that can be easily navigated from any chapter or page as needed. The information is straightforward, helpful, and hopeful. This is just the book I wished for when I became a widow in 2013. In fact, its lessons translate well to any traumatic event. I will keep it handy.

– Kelli Levey Reynolds, Writer

I have read several of Gary's awesome books and recommend them all. This book is different. It is more of a working book. I think it is the best of the best. I hope that I will be able to give it to all my grieving clients.

– Cindy Fanning, LMSW,
Hospice Bereavement Coordinator

Thank you for purchasing

The Grief Guidebook: Common Questions, Compassionate Answers, Practical Suggestions.

These pages are designed to be a companion
for you in your grief journey.

Please don't read this book just once.

Pick it up again in six months or a year.

Come to it again and again.

Each time you will be at a different place.

You'll see your progress. You'll be encouraged.

And you'll find your hope has grown.

As a thanks, please accept this gift – a
free eBook (PDF):

Grief: 9 Things I Wish I Had Known

Download yours today:

**https://www.garyroe.com/
grief-9-things-i-wish-i-had-known-ebook/**

OTHER BOOKS BY GARY ROE

THE COMFORT SERIES

Comfort for Grieving Hearts: Hope and Encouragement in Times of Loss

Comfort for the Grieving Spouse's Heart: Hope and Healing After Losing Your Partner

Comfort for the Grieving Adult Child's Heart: Hope and Healing After Losing Your Parent

Comfort for the Grieving Parent's Heart: Hope and Healing After Losing Your Child

THE GOD AND GRIEF SERIES

Grief Walk: Experiencing God After the Loss of a Loved One

Widowed Walk: Experiencing God After the Loss of a Spouse

THE GOOD GRIEF SERIES

Aftermath: Picking Up the Pieces After a Suicide

Shattered: Surviving the Loss of a Child

Teen Grief: Caring for the Grieving Teenage Heart

Please Be Patient, I'm Grieving: How to Care for and Support the Grieving Heart

Heartbroken: Healing from the Loss of a Spouse

Surviving the Holidays Without You: Navigating Loss During Special Seasons

THE DIFFERENCE MAKER SERIES

Difference Maker: Overcoming Adversity and Turning Pain into Purpose, Every Day (Adult & Teen Editions)

Living on the Edge: How to Fight and Win the Battle for Your Mind and Heart (Adult & Teen Editions)

WHAT THIS BOOK IS ALL ABOUT

Loss strikes. Our hearts are stunned. Our minds reel and spin. Our worlds are shaken.

Over the course of the days and weeks that follow, we begin to discover that life will never be the same. **We** will never be the same.

Someone special is missing.

Questions surface and begin to spill out. We try to make sense of it all. We wonder what this loss will mean for us and our families. We struggle with overwhelming emotions and troubling thoughts. We tussle with what to do and when.

Amid all this upheaval, we long for answers.

Where I'm Coming From

My childhood was riddled with loss. By the time I was a teen, I was wondering if life was worth it. The number and depth of my losses continued to pile up throughout adulthood. My personal pain has spawned question after question along the way.

Over the past three-plus decades, I've had the honor of walking with thousands of grieving hearts through the dark valley of loss. All of them had heartbreaking, gut-wrenching stories of what and who they've lost over the years. The upheaval of such heavy losses can be traumatic and debilitating. I've trudged with them through the endless questions and wonderings.

Over time, I began to see that our questions about loss and grief have patterns to them. We all tend to ask most of the same questions, just in different ways. Amid the coronavirus pandemic, I began hosting "Ask me anything about loss and grief" sessions on Zoom. The response was overwhelming. People came hungry to express what they were struggling with and hear some possible answers and suggestions. During and after these sessions, I received numerous comments and emails saying, "Thank you for doing this!"

After about a year of these sessions, my readers and subscribers convinced me to compile the most common questions I have been asked over the years along with some possible answers and suggestions about how to navigate the difficulties of the grief journey. The result is this book.

How To Read This Book

The Grief Guidebook is designed to meet you where you are in your grief and be a companion for you on your grief journey. Each chapter begins with a grieving heart speaking about the topic or question of that chapter. This is followed by some thoughts about that topic and some possible answers to that question. Each chapter ends with a grief affirmation followed by some possible tips and suggestions for handling that particular grief struggle.

There is no "right" way to read this book. You could move through the book from beginning to end, reading one chapter in each sitting. This allows you to tackle the content a bit at a time and let it soak in. Another approach would be to look at the table of contents and go to those topics you wonder about most. Tackle those first, and then go back through the rest of the book at your own pace.

I am confident you will know how to approach this book in the way that benefits you the most. Look to your heart. Do what makes the most sense to you.

Please take your time. Don't get in a hurry. Grief will not be rushed. This is not a sprint. Pace yourself and let the content in the following pages sink in over time. Good, healthy grieving is about developing habits that bring recovery, healing, hope, and growth.

Once you finish the book, put it somewhere accessible. It can be your grief reference manual from here on. When questions pop up again, as they most certainly will, you can grab this volume and refresh your mind about the possible answers and practical suggestions.

My Hope for You

I wrote this book with the hope that it would bring you some comfort, hope, and healing. I pray that every page has something beneficial that resonates with your mind and heart. Most of all, I hope you hear this message loud and clear: "You are not alone."

You might feel alone, but there are many, many people on the grief road right now. Though our losses are all different, we can still travel this winding path together. We need each other badly.

Breathe deeply. Be kind to yourself. Read on...

Note: You will notice some repetition of key ideas and grief skills throughout this book. This was intentional to emphasize these things and to allow you to read anywhere in the book at any time.

"For in grief nothing "stays put." One keeps on emerging from a phase, but it always recurs. Round and round. Everything repeats. Am I going in circles, or dare I hope I am on a spiral?

But if a spiral, am I going up or down it?

How often -- will it be for always? -- how often will the vast emptiness astonish me like a complete novelty and make me say, "I never realized my loss till this moment"? The same leg is cut off time after time."

**—C.S. Lewis,
A Grief Observed**

PART ONE:

THE EMOTIONAL UPHEAVAL

"This loss has turned my world upside down.
My emotions are intense.
Sometimes, I can barely breathe."

-Sarah

1

HOW COULD THIS HAPPEN?

This can't be real. It just can't.

I can't believe it. It doesn't make any sense.

This is all wrong somehow.

How could this happen?

When we first hear the news of the death of someone we love, our hearts are stunned. Our minds freeze. Even our bodies can go into shock.

Perhaps we start spouting questions. What? Where? When? How? How is this possible? How could this happen to them?

Maybe we're so stunned that nothing comes out of our mouths. We find ourselves wobbly and feeling for a place to sit down. Some of us might faint or become nauseated.

Even if death was expected, nothing could have prepared us for our friend or loved one's final breath. Life always departs in an instant. Even though we knew it was coming, a sense of shock descends upon us.

We are relational creatures. We are interdependent and belong to each other. We get deeply connected. We love and are loved in return. When death invades and suddenly separates us from someone we care about, our hearts writhe in disbelief. Something about this feels wrong somehow. Our hearts scream, "No! How could this happen?"

We don't want this to be real. We don't want to believe it. Our minds can even reason, "If I don't accept this, perhaps it won't be real after all."

Loss is shocking, even if we think we're prepared for it. The death of someone we love is stunning and momentarily paralyzing.

Your heart might be railing against the loss you're experiencing. This initial sense of shock can come and go over the months ahead. Let your heart ask the questions. Give yourself permission to be stunned.

Affirmation:

Loss is shocking. I may have a sense of shock and disbelief about this loss in the months ahead.

Suggestions:

When you're experiencing shock and disbelief, please consider the following:

- Know that this is natural and common. Most grieving hearts go in and out of a sense of shock repeatedly in their grief journey.

- Give yourself permission to be where you are. Accept yourself as you are, in the moment, as best you can. Your heart has been hit. You're stunned.

- Practice taking deep breaths when you can. This is more beneficial than you might think. We'll talk more about the skill of deep breathing later.

Moving in and out of shock is to be expected in the grief process.

2

WHY DOES THIS HURT SO MUCH?

My heart is in such pain. I feel like I'm in pieces.

I've never experienced anything like this.

Why does this hurt so much?

Loss hits our hearts. The pain of losing someone we love can be deep and debilitating.

We are designed for relationship. We come out of the womb screaming for connection. We attach. We are loved, and we learn to love in return. At first, we are dependent. Over time, we become interdependent.

At some point, you attached to your loved one. A special bond was created.

Your loved one was unique in human history. There has never been another person exactly like them, and there never will be again (even if they were a twin). The same is true of you.

This means that your relationship was also one-of-a-kind. Unique. Special. Priceless.

No one can truthfully say, "I know how you feel." No, they don't. They are not you. It wasn't their loved one or their relationship.

Your grief is your own. It is an individual, solitary, and lonely journey.

You were designed for relationship and wired for connection. Separation is painful and can be devastating.

Your pain honors your loved one. When you hurt, you're saying, "I love you."

Affirmation:

Losing someone I love is painful. I give myself permission to hurt and to grieve.

Suggestions:

Grief feels lonely because our loss is one-of-a-kind. When you're hurting, here are some things to consider:

- Please know that the pain you're experiencing is natural and common for those enduring a close, personal loss. Nothing strange is happening. Your heart has been hit and you're feeling the weight of the blow.

- Do your best to accept yourself in the moment and give yourself permission to hurt. This is painful.

- Consider expressing your pain by talking out loud, writing it out in a journal, or sharing with someone you consider safe and trustworthy. Your pain is worthy of attention. You loved the one you lost - and you love them still.

Giving yourself permission to hurt will be important in your grief process.

3

WHY CAN'T I STOP CRYING?

They are always on my mind.

**My emotions are leaking out every-
where. Tears flow all the time.**

It's embarrassing.

Why can't I stop crying?

The loss of someone we care about is sad. Our hearts are feeling their absence. Tears are a natural and healthy expression of what's happening inside.

Grief will not be easily boxed. We can't simply set it aside as something to engage in later. It's not that simple. When our hearts are involved, emotion begins to take up more space in our lives.

When someone we love dies or leaves, it feels like they take a part of us with them. When the separation occurs, a tearing takes place. Imagine two sheets of paper firmly glued together. Separating them again is difficult and messy. The sheet that remains is full of holes. It's still a sheet of paper, but it is significantly different than it was before.

A tearing has occurred. It feels like a part of your heart is now missing. Your world has been altered. You sense that you are no longer the same person. You now have holes that weren't there before.

On top of this, you long for the one you've lost. The pain of the longing can be intense. Sadness can run extremely deep.

Grief will be expressed, one way or another. Better to let it out freely than attempt to stuff it and have it leak out in less than healthy ways.

Feelings are meant to be felt. The sadness is real and deserves expression. Your tears are expressing your affection for the one you've lost.

Let the tears flow.

Affirmation:

Tears are a natural and healthy expression of my sadness. I will allow myself to cry when I want or need to.

Suggestions:

When it comes to tears as an expression of your sadness and grief, here are some things to consider:

- Accept yourself in the moment, as best you can.

- Give yourself permission to grieve, including intense sessions of weeping or sobbing. Your heart has been hit. The emotions are real. Feel the grief and let it out. Let your heart express itself.

- Give yourself the grace to feel intense grief in public places. Most likely, this will happen repeatedly. You are not in control of what you feel and when. Anything can trigger your grief, anytime, anywhere.

- Begin to develop the habit of breathing deeply. This can help calm your mind, heart, and body when powerful emotions are triggered in public places. See the end of chapter five for an explanation of this important grief skill.

Tears are therapeutic and healing. As much as possible, let them come.

4

I CAN'T SEEM TO CRY. WHAT'S WRONG WITH ME?

I don't understand it.

Since their death, I haven't shed a tear. The emotions well up and I can almost feel the wetness behind my eyes, but nothing comes out.

I can't seem to cry. What's wrong with me?

While some grieving hearts can't seem to stop crying, others have trouble crying at all.

Please remember that grief is an individual process. A unique person - you - is suffering through the loss of another unique person and a one-of-a-kind relationship. Although we will have many things in common as grievers, in the end all of us grieve differently.

In other words, grief is not a one-size-fits-all process.

Some people have wept profusely at some losses but can't seem to cry at others. For some of us, the emotions are so strong that our hearts don't know what to do with them. We're afraid that if we start to cry, we'll never be able to stop.

For others, there may be something blocking our tears. A past wound. A traumatic experience. Unresolved conflicts or issues with the one who died. We might still be in shock and unable to release the tears within. Perhaps we don't feel safe enough to cry, for some reason.

Some are disturbed they can sob about other things (like a movie, for instance) yet not weep for their loved one. In such cases, our tears aren't about the movie. The movie simply gave our hearts an opportunity to safely express our grief.

In most cases, as we process our grief in healthy ways over time, our emotions will follow. As we talk, write, and share about our loved one and our relationship with them, our hearts will begin to release what's deep inside.

Do what you can to process this loss in healthy ways. Talk about your loved one with someone you trust. Write about them. Use art to express your heart. Do your best to "get out" what's happening inside you.

Affirmation:

I will refrain from over-analyzing myself and focus on expressing what's happening in my heart in healthy ways.

Suggestions:

If you can't seem to cry and this troubles you, here are some things to consider:

- You are unique. Your loss is one-of-a-kind. Every person is wired somewhat differently. Your grief process is your own.

- Try accepting yourself as you are at present. Be kind to yourself and patient with yourself.

- Connect with someone you trust. Consider sharing with them your concerns and wonderings. It's important to express what's happening inside you.

- Try writing in a journal. A journal is not a diary, but a place to honestly express what's happening inside you. It is a "safe place" where you can share your heart in an authentic and uncensored way.

- In general, focus on expressing your grief in healthy ways. As you do this, the next steps in your grief journey will become apparent along the way.

Let things be what they are in the moment. Accept yourself in the present. Breathe deeply.

5

WHO ELSE AM I GOING TO LOSE?

I can't believe this happened.

If this can happen, then anything can happen to anyone, anywhere, anytime.

I find myself wondering, "Who's next?"

Who else am I going to lose?

One loss usually leads to fear of another. For some, this terror is obvious in our words and actions. For others, our fear of more loss lurks within our hearts and minds.

After the death of someone we love, we look at life and people differently. Life has become unpredictable. The world might seem less safe, more dangerous. We look at the people around us. We naturally begin to wonder what else might happen and to whom.

We become cautious and protective. We find ourselves wanting to take everyone we love and lock them away in a vault somewhere. We start marshaling our energies to make sure that nothing else bad happens to us or to anyone we care about. Instead of saying, "See you soon," we find ourselves admonishing them, "Be careful out there. Stay safe."

Fear is extremely common in grief. Famed writer and scholar C. S. Lewis put it this way after the death of his wife: "No one ever told me that grief felt so like fear."

After a heavy loss, most of us worry about more. We worry about people, finances, adverse circumstances, and potential "what if's." We worry about ourselves and our ability to handle all this. We worry about the future.

Worry naturally leads to fear. Fear in turn fuels worry. Worry sparks more fear, which can morph into terror.

Breathe deeply for a moment. Breathe in through your nose and then out through your mouth. Again. Do this for about a minute.

Now ask yourself the following questions and see which ones resonate best with you:

- What do I find myself focusing on and worrying about?

- What frightens or scares me right now?

- What terrifies me?

Do what you can to process these thoughts. Think about it. Be honest and open with yourself about your fears. Share with someone you trust. Write about these fears in a journal. Work on expressing what's inside you and get these lurking fears out into the open.

You've been hit hard. If you've been hit enough in life, it's natural to wonder when the next blow is coming. "Who else am I going to lose?" is a common question bouncing inside grieving hearts.

Affirmation:

Fear is often a part of grief. I'll be honest with myself about my fears and work on expressing them in healthy ways.

GRIEF SKILL

THE HABIT OF DEEP BREATHING

The habit of deep breathing is an important grief processing skill. Those who practice it regularly have found it extremely helpful in managing the volatile thoughts and emotions that are part of the grief journey.

Breathe in deeply through your nose and then out through your mouth. As an EMT friend of mine says, "Smell the roses, blow out the candle." This activates your parasympathetic nervous system and brings a calming effect to your brain and body.

Breathe deeply and slowly for at least a couple of minutes. Focus as much as possible on your breathing. Close your eyes if necessary.

Consider practicing deep breathing twice a day - once at the beginning of your day and again at the end. As you do this, you're training your mind and body to respond to the intense grief bursts that will come. The more you practice this, the more of a habit deep breathing will become and the easier you'll be able to initiate it when you need it.

Before you read on, practice deep breathing for a few more minutes. Again, this simple skill can be massively beneficial during this time of loss. And the really good news is that anyone can do it, anytime, anywhere.

Breathe.

6

AM I GOING TO DIE? AM I NEXT?

Suddenly, death is personal.

I still can't believe they're gone. It's like they've been stolen in the night.

They were here one minute and gone the next. Life is so fragile.

Am I going to die? Am I next?

———————

The death of someone close to us brings our own mortality into focus. If it could happen to them, it could happen to us.

Our dream of being invincible is crushed. Yes, we knew that we will all die someday, but that day was somewhere far into the future. We were too busy to think about such things. Plus, who wants to think about death?

Now, death has come knocking. It has entered and taken someone we love. Perhaps we still sense death's presence. Many of us begin to wonder about our own death.

A new awareness of our own mortality can bring with it a sense of fear and foreboding. We realize how uncertain

16

and unpredictable life can be. Our illusions of control are shattered.

Fear often produces in us the standard fight-or-flight reflex. We can run from the fear by attempting to shove it down, lock it away, and ignore it. We can immerse ourselves in busyness and activity in the hopes of drowning it out. We might try fighting the fear by staring it down and saying, "You will not get in here. I will not fear. I'm not going to die!"

Both fight and flight reactions lead to the same result: we end up giving the fear more power over us.

Feelings are meant to be felt. Fear is real. When it comes, it is best to acknowledge it. "I'm feeling afraid."

Then try to identify the thought behind the fear. "I'm afraid because I was thinking about how I might die and when."

Once we acknowledge the fear and identify the thought behind it, we can work on releasing it. "I accept that I am fearful - and I choose to release this fear."

The important thing is to begin to accept yourself as you are, in the moment. "I'm scared right now, and that's okay." Once you accept the fear, you begin to unplug its power and influence.

The death of someone you love will naturally bring up thoughts about your own death and any fears associated with that. Accept yourself as best you can, moment by moment.

Affirmation:

It is natural to wonder about my own death. If fear comes, I'll acknowledge it and accept myself as best I can.

Suggestions:

Thinking about your own death can be unnerving or even terrifying. If you find yourself getting fearful or upset, consider doing some of the following:

- Begin breathing deeply. Do this for several minutes. See the last part of the previous chapter for more information on this important grief skill.

- Acknowledge whatever is happening inside you and try to put it into words. Talk out loud or write it down. Express what you're feeling and "get it out."

- Try to identify where these strong emotions are coming from. In other words, what is the thought behind the feeling? "I am afraid because I was thinking about..." Again, express this out loud or write it down. Don't keep it inside.

- Keep breathing deeply and try to accept yourself in the moment. Say out loud, "I'm feeling _____ right now, and that's okay." Again, saying this out loud or writing it down is important.

- Once you've acknowledged what's inside and identified the thoughts behind your emotions, you can continue to process this by talking out loud or writing in a journal. For more information on this, please see the end of chapter 10.

The death of a friend or loved one will most likely raise the issue of your own death or that of others you care about. Accepting yourself and expressing your thoughts and feelings is a huge part of the grief journey.

7

HOW DO I DEAL WITH ANXIETY?

I feel shaky inside.

I'm skittish and nervous.

I'm anxious about everything now.

What is happening to me?

How do I deal with this?

Anxiety is extremely common during times of loss.

Most of us deal with some anxiety on a daily basis. We live in an anxious world. Some of us come from trauma-ridden childhoods and challenging backgrounds. If we're honest, most of us have reason to live in a state of high anxiety.

We all have a somewhat different anxiety baseline. This is the "normal" amount of anxiety we experience and deal with amid routine, everyday life. Some have a higher anxiety baseline than others.

No matter our baseline, however, anxiety naturally increases with a loss. For some of us, a death can send our anxiety soaring off the charts.

Anxiety attacks become common. Panic attacks are not unusual. Ongoing high anxiety plagues many grieving hearts.

When anxiety strikes, we feel hijacked. Something invades and takes us over. We feel ourselves losing control. It feels like our own minds and bodies are betraying us. We can think we're losing it or going crazy.

The reality is that our hearts have been hit hard by the death of someone we love. Our worlds have been forcefully altered. We live in a different world now, one without our friend or loved one. All the change is staggering and unnerving. Anxiety is the natural result.

When anxiety comes, breathe deeply. It's important to breathe in through your nose and out through your mouth. This activates your parasympathetic nervous system and sends a calming message to your brain. If you can, practice deep breathing several times a day when you're not anxious. The more your practice, the better able you will be to initiate this helpful skill when you need it most.

Acknowledge and accept the anxiety. "I'm feeling anxious, and that's okay." Identify, if you can, the thought behind the anxiety. "I'm feeling anxious because I'm wondering about the future." The more you accept the anxiety and where it's coming from, the less power it will have.

Fleeing the anxiety is not helpful. Fighting it is fruitless. Both roads only give the anxiety more power and influence. Instead, accept it. By accepting the anxiety, you unplug its dread. Tell yourself, "I'm anxious and that's okay. I'm grieving."

Affirmation:

I'll remember that anxiety is natural and common in grief. I'll accept the anxiety when it comes and accept myself in the moment as best I can.

Suggestions:

When you find yourself getting anxious, please consider implementing the following tips.

- Begin breathing deeply. Do this for several minutes. This will help calm your mind and heart so that you can begin to process what you're feeling and thinking. Please see the end of chapter five for a more detailed explanation of the skill of deep breathing.

- Acknowledge the anxiety. Try to identify the thoughts that led to this anxiety spike. Express this out loud or in writing.

- Accept where you are in the moment. Tell yourself, "I'm anxious right now, and that's okay. I'm grieving."

Increased anxiety is extremely common on the grief journey. When anxiety comes, acknowledge it, express it, and accept it as part of your grief process.

GRIEF SKILL

A.I.R. YOUR EMOTIONS

Acronyms can help us remember some of the key skills we'll need in our grief process. "A.I.R." is one I use to help with processing emotions.

A - Acknowledge

The first step is to acknowledge what you're feeling. "I'm feeling sad." "I'm feeling scared." "I'm feeling anxious." Express this to yourself out loud or write it down. Acknowledging what's happening inside you begins to slow down the internal spinning that can often disturb us.

I - Identify

After acknowledging what you're feeling, try to identify the thought behind that emotion. "I'm sad because I was thinking about..." "I'm feeling anxious because I was thinking about..." Don't get caught in overanalyzing and overthinking this. Go with what comes to mind.

Again, express this out loud and / or write it down. This also slows the mind and heart down long enough to give you some relief and to help you process what is happening inside you.

R - Release

Once you've acknowledged the emotion and identified the thought or thoughts behind it, begin breathing deeply. Close your eyes. See yourself releasing the feelings and thoughts you've identified. Some find it helpful to have their hands clenched into fists and then open them, symbolizing this release. Others picture themselves breathing out their thoughts and feelings.

Acknowledge, identify, and release. This may seem awkward at first. As you practice this and repeatedly A.I.R. your emotions, this process can become an invaluable habit on this difficult journey through loss.

Do you have to do it exactly like this? No, of course not. Everyone is different. Stay flexible and open. Do what you can to intentionally process your grief. "Get it out" in healthy ways.

8

WHAT DO I DO WITH THE ANGER I FEEL?

I'm angry about what happened.

Surely someone could have done something.

Why did this have to happen?
Why do we have to die?

What do I do with this anger?

Anger is a powerful emotion. It is a natural and common part of the grief process.

Almost everyone experiences anger of some kind during times of loss. Someone important to us is no longer here. Our lives have been disrupted and upended. Since we're relational and wired for connection, our hearts wince and writhe against the loss.

Anger looks for a target. We begin looking for someone to blame. Who is responsible for this? Who messed up? Who could have intervened and didn't?

We might blame those around the person when they died. We could hold medical staff or other professionals responsible. We could turn the anger on ourselves. We might even blame the deceased. Many blame God.

Anger is natural. Though it's a powerful emotion, it's not inherently negative. Emotions in their essence are neutral. It's what we choose to do with them that ends up being negative or positive, unhealthy or healthy.

Anger will be expressed, one way or another. See it as part of your grief and seek proactive healthy ways to "get it out."

Here are some options:

- Exercise! This is a wonderful means of taking the edge off our anger.

- Scream out loud (in private, of course).

- Punch a pillow or use a punching bag.

- Express your anger in writing - journal, letters, poetry, etc.

- Express your anger through art - drawing, painting, etc.

- Breathe deeply and see yourself blowing the anger out.

Anger that is not purposefully expressed in healthy ways will eventually leak out in ways that you will most likely regret.

Take your anger seriously. Acknowledge it. "I'm angry." Identify the thought behind it if you can. "I'm angry because I am powerless to bring my loved one back!" Accept the anger as best you can.

As you accept and process your anger, you will learn and grow from it rather than being controlled by it.

Affirmation:

If anger comes, I will acknowledge and accept it as a natural part of my grief. As I express my anger in healthy ways, I will heal and grow.

Suggestions:

Anger is a challenging emotion for all of us. Expressing it in healthy ways to keep it from festering inside can be a challenge. Here are some tips for you when anger surfaces.

- When you feel angry, begin breathing deeply. This can help calm you to the point where you can begin to express your anger in a healthy way. For more information on the skill of deep breathing, see the end of chapter five.

- After you're a little calmer, begin to A.I.R. (acknowledge, identify, release) your anger. Acknowledge it. "I feel angry right now." Try to identify the thoughts behind that anger. "I'm feeling angry because I was just thinking about..." Then begin to release that anger. Keep breathing deeply and see yourself "blowing the anger out." See it drifting up and away from you. Or picture your anger as something in your hands and clench your fists. Breathe deeply and open your hands and release that anger. Check the end of the previous chapter for a detailed description of what it means to A.I.R. your emotions.

- Sometimes your anger might seem to demand more physical expression. If so, try one of the bullet points previously listed in this chapter.

- Make the commitment to - as much as possible - process and A.I.R. the anger as it comes. Don't put it off and allow it to build up inside. You don't need any extra burdens.

Experiencing anger in some form while grieving is extremely common. Process the anger as it comes. "Get it out" in healthy ways.

9

HOW DO I DEAL WITH ALL THE GUILT I FEEL?

I feel guilty.

**I should have known. I should have
said or done something different.**

I said and did things I shouldn't have.

I messed up. I'm to blame.

It's my fault.

How do I deal with all the guilt I feel?

————————————

Our anger looks for a target. Often, the most convenient target is ourselves.

None of us are perfect. We all have regrets. When someone dies, however, we look back and see mistakes and omissions. We become hyper-conscious of what we wish we had or had not said or done. Unable yet to release our loved one, we concoct things that we could have said or done that might have made a difference somehow.

Guilt is the result.

Most of us are quite familiar with guilt. Many of us have known it well since childhood. It invaded our lives early and began to exert its influence. It whispered its accusations into our small, impressionable minds and hearts. It took up residence in our lives and has been a continual player in our lives ever since.

When loss strikes, guilt recognizes a prime opportunity to strengthen its position. "Look at what you did or didn't do. Look at the terrible, tragic result. You've really blown it this time."

Guilt wants control. If we listen to it, our hearts begin trending toward hopelessness and despair.

Guilt benefits no one. It is not our friend. Its voice does not help us grieve well, honor our loved one, or love anyone around us. Guilt is an emotional boa that slowly and efficiently squeezes the life right out of us.

When guilt comes, acknowledge it. "I'm feeling guilty."

Identify the thought behind the guilt. "I'm feeling guilty because I'm thinking that..."

Release the guilt as best you can. The more you do this, the more guilt will get the message that it is no longer welcome.

If you honestly see yourself as responsible for something related to your friend or loved one's death, then being able to process that and forgive yourself is hugely important. More on that later...

Affirmation:

Guilt is not my friend. When it comes, I'll acknowledge the guilt and then release it as best I can.

Suggestions:

Guilt is a common visitor in the grief process. Dealing with it well can be difficult and frustrating. Here are some suggestions to consider when this unwelcome invader comes knocking on your heart.

- When you sense guilt's presence, begin to A.I.R. that emotion. Acknowledge the guilt. Identify the thoughts behind it. "I'm feeling guilty because I was just thinking about..." And then do your best to release it. Breathe deeply and see yourself breathing out the guilt. Or picture the guilt clenched in your fists, and then open your hands and release it. For more information on the A.I.R. Grief skill, please see the end of chapter seven.

- When it comes to guilt, many find writing or journaling to be helpful. Consider taking some time to write about what you're feeling and why. A.I.R. your guilt on paper (or type it out on a screen).

- You might even want to make a "guilt list." Jot down the things you feel guilty about. Good prompts for this are, "if only I had..." And "I wish I hadn't..."

- Guilt tends to be persistent. Set your mind to deal with it every time it surfaces. As you practice handling guilt, you're building good grief habits that will help you in other areas too.

Guard your heart by processing guilt when it surfaces. Keep releasing it, as many times as necessary.

10

HOW DO I HANDLE EMOTIONAL OVERWHELM?

I wake up shaking. Intense feelings descend upon me even before I open my eyes.

A heavy cloud of emotion surrounds me all day long. Thankfully, I get a few breaks here and there.

Honestly, I'm overwhelmed. It's like I've turned into one big mass of grief.

Is this normal?

I need help. How do I handle this emotional overwhelm?

We all need help. We're relational creatures wired for connection. None of us can do this alone.

Almost all grieving hearts experience times of emotional overwhelm. Our emotions become so strong that they take over. Grief seems to be taking up more and more of our hearts, minds, and lives. At times, it might even feel like grief's roller-coaster emotions are all that's left of us.

Grieving the loss of a close friend or loved one is emotionally, mentally, physically, and even spiritually exhausting. We move through the day encased in a cloud of grief. This emotional roller coaster is unpredictable, with dizzying climbs, drops, and sharp, sudden turns. We get jostled and thrown about frequently.

At times, we're hanging on for dear life, wondering when this bumpy, scary, and even terrifying ride will be over.

The first key to handling emotional overwhelm is to accept yourself as you are and your grief as it is. Your life has been upended and your heart is desperately trying to find its balance. Though frustrating, confusing, and scary, emotional overwhelm is part of the grief process.

The simple skill of breathing deeply can be huge at these times. This skill of breathing in deeply through your nose and then out through your mouth needs to be practiced frequently when you're not in a state of overwhelm. The more ingrained and familiar this skill becomes, the easier you'll be able to initiate it when you need it.

When you find yourself emotionally overwhelmed, do what you can to process what's happening inside you. Simply put, "get the grief out" any way you can - in healthy ways, of course. Talk it out. Write it out. Art it out. These emotions will be expressed, one way or another. As you intentionally "let them out" in healthy ways, the internal emotional pressure will most likely subside.

Connecting with someone you trust who knows grief well can be extremely helpful. A seasoned grief veteran can bring perspective and wisdom. Just being heard and understood can do wonders for an overwhelmed grieving heart.

Be kind to yourself. Accept yourself as best you can. Episodes of emotional overwhelm are common in grief.

Affirmation:

When I'm emotionally overwhelmed, I'll be kind to myself and accept myself as best I can. Overwhelm is natural and common while grieving the loss of someone special.

GRIEF SKILL

T.W.A.:
TALK IT OUT. WRITE IT OUT.
ART IT OUT.

Here's another important grief skill. I call this grief pro-
cessing method T.W.A. That used to stand for Trans-World
Airlines (now long gone). Here, T.W.A. stands for "Talk,
Write, Art."

This skill, simply put, is about helping you "get the grief
out." There's a grief reservoir in all of us. It's raining on
this reservoir all the time. Sometimes it's a drizzle, while
other times it's a downpour. Grief flash floods are also
common. If we don't have ways to "open our spillway"
and let some of the grief out, it ends up overflowing and
controlling all of life.

T.W.A. is one way to open the spillways of our grief
reservoir - and keep them open.

T - Talk it out.

"T" stands for "talk it out." Talk out loud to yourself.
Share with someone safe that you can trust and who
listens well. Talk.

Talking forces our minds and hearts to slow down
enough to put our thoughts and emotions into words.
When we talk out loud, we hear our own voice, which
is more important than we might realize. When we

talk, we're consciously expressing what's happening inside us as it's happening.

W - Write it out.

"W" stands for "write it out." Write it out in a journal. Write it out in a letter, poem, or story. Get what's happening inside you out and on paper (or a screen). Writing also slows our spinning thoughts and swirling emotions and helps focus us. We're physically involved too - writing or typing. We're reading what we've written as we go. All of this naturally helps us process the grief within.

A - Art it out.

"A" stands for "art it out." Draw how you're feeling. Paint, sculpt, or craft what's happening inside you. Be creative.

There's something about art that touches us on a different level. Art can be an excellent and positive way to open our spillways and release some of our grief. Engaging our creativity is immensely helpful in processing loss.

Chances are you'll prefer one of these above the other two. That's just fine. We all have our preferences. Work with the one that seems most comfortable but try not to forget the other two. All three combined in some form can become important tools in your grief toolbox.

Open the spillways of your grief reservoir. Talk it out. Write it out. Art it out.

11

WHY DON'T I FEEL LIKE MYSELF ANYMORE?

I feel so different now. Nothing is the same.

I'm easily overwhelmed – by my own emotions, by people, and by situations.

I can hardly seem to handle anything anymore.

What's happening? Why don't I feel like myself anymore?

Have I lost myself too?

After a loss, we feel different because the world has changed. Our personal world has taken a titanic shift. Someone we love is missing. Their absence permeates everything now.

Powerful emotions surge up and pound us. Sadness, anger, fear, and guilt are continually shouting at us, seemingly all at once. People treat us differently. The rest of the world zips along without missing a beat. Every part of our being – heart, mind, body, and soul – are feeling the shock of this loss.

Our usual routine is gone. No wonder we don't feel like ourselves.

We don't yet realize it, but this loss is changing us. It must. We can't remain the same people we were, and we would not want to. What would it say about us if we endured the loss of a beloved family member or friend and then went right on as the same people we were before?

Impossible. We have hearts. We attach. We love. Through all of this, we learn and grow. When loss occurs, our hearts must eventually find their way to adjust, learn, recover, heal, and grow through the grief process.

As we process our grief in healthy ways, we will heal, but we will not be the same as we once were.

Change is hard, and yet necessary. Change takes energy, courage, and humility. We must be willing to stretch, to be uncomfortable, and to go through pain and upset. If we're willing, loss and this arduous grief journey can teach us how to live with even more passion and purpose than before.

If you don't feel like the same person since your loss, it's because you're not the same. You are changing – adjusting, recovering, and healing.

Embrace the grief process. Find good mentors and trustworthy companions. Set your heart to honor your loved one by learning to live even better than before.

Affirmation:

I don't feel the same because I'm not the same anymore. I will honor my loved one by learning to adjust, recover, heal, grow, and live with more purpose than ever.

Suggestions:

When you don't feel like yourself, consider trying some of the things below.

- Make a list of what's different in your life since your loss. Be specific. Don't censor yourself.

- Now ask yourself, "How am I different since this loss?" Write down what comes to mind.

- As you look at these two lists, it will become apparent that your world and life have changed. You're now dealing with these changes. No wonder you don't feel like your old self.

- You need trustworthy companions and mentors on your grief journey. Does anyone come to mind?

Give yourself permission to feel "different" or even "weird" during this time of loss and adjustment. Things have shifted, and you are shifting to meet all these new challenges.

12

WHY IS GRIEF SO CONFUSING?

I thought life was one way, and now it's another.

My old life is gone. Where? I don't know.

**My good friend is gone and took
my heart with them.**

I don't know which way is up. I feel strange. Weird.

Why is grief so confusing?

For a moment, picture your life as a large spiderweb. Each strand of the web represents one of your relationships. Every strand is different.

Some strands are short, small, and thin, while others by comparison are long, large and thick.

Some strands are central to the entire web, while others are peripheral.

Some strands are strong, while others appear frail and weak.

Now, imagine that one of your strong, thick, central strands was suddenly severed. What would happen?

At best, your entire web would shake. At worst, the web would collapse on itself and be almost unrecognizable.

An important strand of your web has been severed. Your entire web is trembling with the shock. If the strand was central enough, you might even feel like your web is collapsing.

This is disorienting. Everything feels strange. Nothing is quite the same because you are no longer the same. Your web is different now.

The sheer number of changes that occur in your life from one loss is staggering. It's like you've been transported to a different world - an alternate universe - but almost everything looks the same. But it's not the same. It's a different world for you.

That's confusing.

If your world feels strange and surreal at present, please know that this is very common for grieving hearts. Breathe deeply. When massive change occurs, things naturally feel weird for a while - perhaps for quite some time.

Affirmation:

Things can be confusing because so much has changed. I'll breathe deeply and accept that this confusing weirdness is part of the grief process.

Suggestions:

Loss can be disorienting. Here are a few tips for dealing with the natural confusion that comes with a close loss.

- When you become aware that you're feeling confused, take a few minutes and breathe deeply. Take your time. Focus on your breathing. See the end of chapter five for a step-by-step description of this grief skill.

- When you're ready, A.I.R. your confusion. Acknowledge it. Then identify the thoughts behind it. "I feel confused because I'm thinking about..." Consider talking out loud or writing this out. Then, when you sense you've processed it a little, try to release the confusion. Let it pass on through. For more information on what it means to A.I.R. your emotions, please see the end of chapter seven.

- Consider sharing your sense of confusion and frustration with someone you trust. Being honest and sharing what's happening inside you can be unnerving, but good. Your heart needs to be seen and heard by others who will take your pain and grief seriously.

Loss can be disorienting. Be kind to yourself. Talk it out. Write it out. Art it out.

13

IS IT OKAY TO FEEL NUMB?

At first, I felt everything.

Now, I have trouble feeling anything.

It's like my heart shut down.

Am I going to be okay? Is it normal to feel numb?

To say that loss is emotional is a gross understatement. The emotional upheaval is one of the first things we notice about the grief process.

We've said before when loss hits the heart, emotion begins to spill out everywhere. The volume and intensity of the emotions can be overwhelming.

Sometimes, however, the emotional weight can become too heavy. The heart can't take any more at the moment, and our "feelers" begin to shut down. We can become numb for a time.

This numbness can be for our own protection. If we were to ever feel the full weight of the intensity of our grief, it might kill us.

When an electrical circuit is overloaded, a breaker gets tripped and the flow of electricity is cut off to prevent damage. Gas stations are equipped with emergency fuel stop buttons that shut off all pumps in case of a fire or accident. In the same way, our heart's "feelers" can shut down when overloaded. This gives our hearts and minds a grief break.

Experiencing some numbness after a loss is common. Most grievers indicate that they "shut down" at some time in their grief journey. Some go in and out of feeling numb as time goes on.

Going numb doesn't mean you don't care. It doesn't mean you didn't love the deceased. Numbness isn't an indication that you are insensitive, unfeeling, or that your heart has departed. Numbness is a temporary break - an emotional rest period - from the overwhelming intensity of the loss.

If you're numb at present, rest assured your heart is still there. The emotions will return. Keep breathing deeply and accept the numbness as part of your grief process.

Loss and grief clearly teach us that things change. Life is always in flux. Now is not forever. The numbness will change too.

Affirmation:

**If I go numb for a while, I'll accept it
as part of my grief. When I'm ready,
my heart will begin to feel again.**

Suggestions:

In times of heavy grief, you might sense your feelers shutting down. Here are a few things to consider when grief numbness strikes.

- Tell yourself, "This is where I am. I'm grieving and my heart is overloaded." Accepting yourself is the first step in healthy grieving.

- Consider using T.W.A. to process this present numbness (see the end of chapter 10 for a detailed explanation). Acknowledge the numbness. What thoughts are currently running through your mind? What concerns you about where you are at present? Are there worries or fears burdening you? Talk about it, write it out, or use art to process it. Again, the focus is simply "getting the grief out."

- Consider sharing what you're experiencing with someone who knows grief well. This might be a friend, family member, coworker, or even a grief professional (grief counselor, grief therapist, hospice bereavement staff, support group facilitator, pastor, etc.). Your grieving heart needs to feel seen and heard during this process.

- If you haven't already embraced the practice of deep breathing as a key grief skill, please consider doing so (see the end of chapter five for more information). This simple practice can make a massive difference in helping you navigate this loss and the resulting grief.

Grief can be heavy enough that your feelers shut down for periods of time. Your mind and heart need rest during this exhausting journey.

14

IS IT NORMAL TO BE DEPRESSED AFTER A DEATH?

I feel so down.

I don't want to do anything or go anywhere. I don't want to see anyone.

Nothing sounds good.

Am I depressed? I feel depressed.

Is it normal to be depressed after a death?

Depression used to carry a huge stigma. Over time, we've finally gotten to the point where it's commonly accepted that depression is something that many experience.

Technically speaking, feeling depressed and being seriously depressed are two different things. We can have plenty of reasons to feel depressed. The death of someone we love is certainly one of those.

Almost all grieving hearts experience some depression. This depression is usually temporary and situational. In other words, it's directly related to the death of our friend or loved one. In the grief journey, we can feel depressed repeatedly, for various lengths of time.

If we're wondering if what we're feeling is "normal" or "okay," we can ask ourselves this question: Does what I'm feeling fit what's happening? In other words, are my emotions congruent with the loss I'm experiencing?

Does feeling depressed fit the death of a friend or loved one? Is it congruent with what's happening? Yes. Absolutely.

If you haven't already, you will most likely experience some extreme sadness or temporary depression in your grief journey. If the depression continues and deepens to the point that it concerns you, please seek the advice of a qualified professional.

As you take your heart seriously and process your grief in healthy ways, these episodes of temporary depression will most likely resolve. Though everything might seem drab and lifeless at times, the color will return.

Affirmation:

It's okay if I experience some temporary depression. This loss-related depression will resolve over time as I process my grief in healthy ways.

Suggestions:

Most grieving hearts experience some temporary grief depression during times of loss. When feelings of depression descend upon you, here are a few tips to consider.

- Own up to your present reality. Acknowledge the depression. Accept yourself as best you can. Self-acceptance can lead to healthy responses, whereas fighting against the depression or attempting to flee from it only gives it more power and influence.

- Ask yourself the following questions. Is it okay to feel depressed? Do your emotions seem to match the loss you've experienced? Can you think of some healthy ways you can express this grief depression you're feeling? Consider using T.W.A. (talk it out, write it out, art it out) to help. See the end of chapter 10 for more info on T.W.A.

- Exercise can make a big difference with grief-related temporary depression. Movement and moderate, appropriate exercise boosts your wellness and releases much-needed endorphins.

- Practice good self-care in terms of nutrition and hydration. Extra sugar and carbs tend to fuel depression rather than helping. We often eat for comfort, yet the comfort we seek through food is fleeting at best. In the end, eating well and staying hydrated can elevate your mood and contribute to your overall wellness.

Temporary, situational depression is common for those on the grief journey. Let your heart express itself.

15

AM I GOING CRAZY?

I feel sad, angry, and depressed.

I feel confused, lonely, and exhausted.

Nothing feels right. I feel strange.

I feel like I'm losing it at times.

Am I going crazy?

———————

At some point in the grief journey, most people wonder if they're going crazy.

The incredible amount of emotional upheaval combined with various life changes packed into a short period of time can be disorienting and confusing. It's as if our lives have been turned upside down. We can wonder which end is up.

Change is the one constant in the grief process. Change, change, and more change. We began experiencing these changes from the time we knew death was coming. If the death was sudden, change began at that moment.

We quickly discover that the death itself was just one loss of many. Soon after our friend or loved one is gone, more losses start to cascade down upon us. We not only lose the person, but everything in our lives attached to them as well. A loss domino effect occurs. We can bump into a new loss almost every day - even multiple times a day.

Our grief is never about one loss. It's about all the losses that occur over time resulting from the death of our friend or loved one.

No wonder we feel crazy at times.

Does what you're experiencing seem to fit the heaviness and complexity of all the losses you're enduring? Probably so. Are your feelings, thoughts, and actions congruent with the incredible stress of all the change you're having to manage? Most likely, yes.

So, chances are you're not crazy. You are, however, in a crazy situation compared to your old life and routine. The loss and all the ensuing upheaval might be crazy, but you're not.

Breathe deeply. Accept yourself where you are, as you are. Be kind to yourself. This is painful, hard, confusing, and even disorienting.

Affirmation:

I'll remember that feeling a little crazy is common in grief. I'm not crazy, but life is crazy-different now because of this loss.

Suggestions:

Many grieving hearts question their sanity on their grief journey. Here are a few things that might help when you're wondering if you're losing it.

- Think for a moment about how much has changed for you since your loss. Consider making a list: "Things that are different now." Be as specific as you can.

- Is there someone you trust that you can share freely with - without fear of judgment? If so, consider telling them how you feel and some of what's roaming around in your mind. You might ask them beforehand to just listen. Let them know you're not looking for advice. Simply expressing your heart to another person can be relieving and comforting.

- If you're wondering whether what you're experiencing is "normal," you might want to consider reaching out to someone who knows grief well or a grief professional. Local hospices, religious organizations, and healthcare services often have knowledgeable, experienced people ready and willing to listen and walk alongside you in this.

All the change and upheaval you're enduring can make you question your sanity. Give yourself time and space to grieve. You will get through this, one day at a time.

16

HOW DO I DEAL WITH GRIEF ATTACKS?

Grief is crazy.

I'll be fine, and then not fine.

All of a sudden, the grief will be on me like a tiger.

Powerful feelings can overtake and overwhelm me in a nanosecond.

These grief attacks are terrifying and embarrassing.

How do I deal with them?

Grief attacks, or grief bursts, are extremely common after a loss.

The problem is that we might never have experienced such an attack before. It's new to us, and therefore frightening and unnerving.

I don't like the word "attack" much in this case. I prefer "burst" because "attack" has a negative, you-need-to-protect-yourself connotation to it.

The truth is that grief "bursts" are perfectly natural and healthy. Grief doesn't come from the outside. Our grief is within us, and it tends to build up over time.

We're walking along minding our own business and then it happens. We feel the grief rising rapidly inside. Powerful, intense emotion overwhelms us.

Many times, there is a trigger of some kind - a song, an aroma, a person, a place, etc. The grief within is triggered and some internal pressure gets suddenly released.

Grief bursts don't need a trigger, however. Sometimes they just happen.

We can't run from these bursts. They will catch us. We can't fight them either. They're already on us before we know it.

We don't like them because we feel out of control. But we're never in control, really. We don't like grief bursts because we feel embarrassed and self-conscious. But when we're grieving, we're already self-conscious and always on the verge of embarrassment.

Again, grief bursts are natural, extremely common, and healthy. They are to be welcomed and embraced.

What do you do when a grief burst comes? If possible, ride it out. Let the grief come. Allow yourself to express the emotions.

If you're in certain public places, this can be frightening. You can be proactive and have an exit strategy beforehand. If a grief burst strikes, what will you do?

Here are three possible exit strategies:

- Option A: I'll breathe deeply and try to stay where I am and ride it out.

- Option B: I'll excuse myself to a more private location where I can express my emotions.

- Option C: I'll acknowledge the grief burst but put it on hold. When I'm alone, I'll process the event further.

There is no right or wrong to this. You will not be able to get this perfect. It's about learning, healing, and growing by processing your grief well.

Affirmation:

When grief bursts come, I'll embrace them and process the emotions in healthy ways. I'll remember these bursts are natural, common, and healthy.

Suggestions:

Grief bursts will come. Here are a few tips on how you can prepare for grief spikes in the future.

- Think about the week ahead. Where and when is your grief likely to be triggered this week? Pick one possible place and time. Imagine yourself there. Consider the three possible exit strategies in this chapter. Which one (Option A, B, or C) sounds best to you in this situation?

- Consider taking some time each morning to think through your day beforehand. If there are appointments, people, or situations that you anticipate might be difficult, plan your exit strategy in case you need it. Just the sense of being prepared will decrease some of the potential dread involved.

- Either during or immediately after a grief burst, consider using A.I.R. to process your way through it (see the end of chapter seven for a detailed explanation). Be honest with yourself and acknowledge whatever you're feeling. Identify the thoughts that are running through your mind. And then do your best to release those emotions and thoughts.

- After a grief burst, take a few moments and debrief yourself from the experience. How did it go? What do you wish you had done differently? What can you learn from that experience?

Grief bursts will come. Proactively plan for them. Your grief bursts honor the one you lost.

17

IS IT NORMAL TO FEEL VULNERABLE AFTER A LOSS?

I was confident before.

I felt competent and stable.

Now I feel unsteady and unsure.

I'm hesitant and cautious.

I feel vulnerable.

Is it normal to feel this way after a loss?

If our heart is hit hard enough - if the loss is close and powerful enough - we're naturally knocked off our feet. The blow is dizzying and disorienting. We lie there and gasp for breath.

As we slowly crawl to our knees, we can already sense that the world is different. Something staggering has happened. A one-of-a-kind person we cared about and loved is gone. A strand of our life web has been severed. Everything is shaking now. We're naturally stunned. When we manage to stand, we sway and stagger.

A natural result of all of this is a new feeling of vulnerability. The world and life suddenly feel unpredictable, uncertain, and even dangerous. Our minds are grappling with the fact that anything can happen to anyone at any time. No wonder we feel vulnerable.

We feel vulnerable because we **are** vulnerable. We are not invincible. We are not impervious or all-powerful. We are not in control of what happens to us or around us. The sudden recognition of the extent of our vulnerability can be startling and even terrifying.

Yes, it's common and natural to feel vulnerable - more vulnerable - during this time of loss and grief.

When we feel vulnerable, our first reflex is to try to take control of something, preferably as much as possible. We tell people what to do. We try to fix problems and upsets. We become obsessive about certain parts of our lives and routines. We make impulsive decisions. We try to protect ourselves and those we love any way we can.

Our attempts to take control might feel good at times, but they are rarely helpful or successful. What tends to work better and be healthier for our hearts is accepting this new sense of vulnerability. As we own up to what's happening inside us and begin to "let it out" and express it in healthy ways (see the description of T.W.A. at the end of chapter 10), our hearts will usually settle a bit.

As we accept what is, though it be uncomfortable and scary, we can begin to respond rather than simply react. When we attempt to run from or fight against what is, we end up adding fuel to the fires of fear, anxiety, and depression.

Feeling vulnerable while grieving is natural and common. Accepting yourself where you are is important.

Affirmation:

Feeling vulnerable is part of grieving. Rather than trying to control someone or something, I'll accept myself as I am, where I am.

Suggestions:

Here are some tips for when you're feeling vulnerable.

- Practice breathing deeply (see the end of chapter five for more info). Deep breathing can slow down your mind and heart so that you're better able to process what's happening inside you.

- Remind yourself that it's okay to feel vulnerable. Vulnerability is not weakness. It's a universal human condition. We are not invincible. We have hearts. Sometimes our hearts get broken.

- Identify and make a list of what you tend to feel vulnerable about. Your health, appearance, relationships, job, emotions, finances, future, parenting, marriage, etc. Simply being honest with yourself and "getting it out" can be helpful and relieving.

- Consider sharing with someone you trust. You can use your list to guide your sharing.

Resist thinking that hiding or faking it is a sign of strength. Grieving well with courage requires being real about what's going on inside you.

18

IS APATHY A PART OF GRIEF?

I sigh a lot now.

I find myself thinking and even saying, "Whatever."

**If this can happen, if we all die,
then what's the point?**

Frankly, I don't care anymore, and that scares me.

Do other people experience this?

Is apathy a part of grief?

Most grieving hearts experience at least some apathy in their grief journey.

Our hearts have been hit so hard that sometimes our "feelers" have to shut down. We can become numb at times (see chapter 13). Loss stirs questions and wonderings in our hearts. One question that often surfaces is, "What's the point of all this anyway?"

Though that question might be scary, it's often one the heart needs to ask. We need to know why we're here and what life is all about. If we don't, we'll end up simply doing what everyone else does and going through the motions chasing things that in the end really don't matter much.

If we've had heavy, serious losses in the past, this loss can push us into apathy. If close and deep enough, this loss all by itself can drive us into the land of "Whatever."

Whatever Land is a temporary rest stop along the grief journey, not a permanent destination. We pass through Whatever Land but don't make a home there.

We don't do well without a clear sense of meaning and purpose. Recognizing apathy and processing it are important.

If you find yourself feeling apathetic, please know that this is natural and common for a grieving heart. Let your heart express itself and ask the questions it needs to.

Be aware that part of the apathy you experience could be coming from anger toward yourself, others, God, or the world in general. Owning up to and processing that anger is healthy for your mind and heart. Don't let it hide, fester, and infect your life and relationships in adverse ways.

When in Whatever Land, be aware of what you're thinking and feeling. Know that most grieving hearts experience some apathy on this journey. See yourself accepting where you are in Whatever Land, but also know that you are passing through.

Be kind to yourself. This is hard.

Affirmation:

If I'm feeling apathetic, I'll be real with myself about that. I'll remember that Whatever Land is a temporary stop and not a permanent residence.

Suggestions:

When you're feeling apathetic, here are some tips that might help.

- Accept yourself where you are as you are. Now is not forever. Things will change.

- When apathy comes, process it well. "Get it out" by practicing T.W.A. (talk it out, write it out, art it out). For an explanation of T.W.A., please see the end of chapter 10.

- Visualize yourself in apathy-filled Whatever Land. Notice what comes to mind. What do you see? What's happening there? What are you doing? See Whatever Land for what it is - a temporary stop on the grief journey. See yourself passing on through.

See apathy for what it is - a temporary stop along the grief road. As you express your grief in healthy ways, you'll find yourself passing on through Whatever Land.

19

AM I GOING TO MAKE IT THROUGH THIS?

**I would never have thought loss and
grief would be so painful and hard.**

I've never felt like this.

I've never been through anything like this.

This is awful.

I feel empty, lost, and alone.

Am I going to make it through this?

––––––––––––––

The loss of someone special can be so deep and painful
that we can wonder if we're going to survive it.

We've experienced other losses before. We might even
think we're old hands at this and know how to navigate
grief. And then we get hit again and somehow everything
is different.

Every person is unique. Every relationship is one-of-
a-kind. Every loss has its own grief journey. Some of the
terrain might look familiar, but this part of the path is new
to us.

Many feel empty and lost after the death of a close friend or loved one. This is common and natural. Someone has exited our lives. Their physical presence is gone. A hole opens up in our hearts and lives. No wonder we experience a sense of emptiness inside. We're feeling the new hole within.

We begin to navigate the path in front of us by being real about what's happening in our hearts and process our emotions and thoughts in healthy ways.

We do our best to accept reality as it is and ourselves as we are.

We connect with safe, trustworthy people for support, encouragement, and perspective.

We guard our hearts by limiting our exposure to unhelpful or even toxic influences.

We journey this obstacle-ridden, seemingly always uphill path one day, one hour, one minute, one step at a time.

You've lost someone special. You will never get over this because you will always miss them on some level. Love endures. You will get through this, but you will never be the same. You will heal, adjust, recover, and grow.

And if you're willing, this loss can teach you to live with even more compassion, love, and meaning than ever before.

Affirmation:

I am on the grief journey. I will get through this tumultuous and painful time, one day, one hour, one minute, one step at a time.

Suggestions:

Ultimately, we can only live life one step at a time. Here are some tips to help you live life more in the present moment.

- Practice the skill of deep breathing (see chapter five for a detailed explanation). This skill brings your attention back to the present moment. Take a few minutes once or twice a day and breathe in deeply through your nose and out through your mouth. Focus on your breathing and let everything else fade into the background.

- When you feel upset, sad, anxious, angry, fearful, or guilty, consider taking a few minutes and A.I.R. that emotion (see chapter seven for more info). Acknowledge what you're feeling. Identify the thought behind that emotion. Then release these thoughts and feelings as best you can. As you A.I.R. your emotions, you become more connected to the present moment.

- Think for a moment about the people and influences in your life. Are any of them unhelpful or even toxic to you right now? How might you guard your heart by limiting your exposure to some of the things and people that tend to drag you down?

- Do you have safe people in your life? Do you have some people who listen and support you well? Consider touching base with one safe person every day. Call, text, email, or get together. Simple contact with healthy people can make a huge difference in your grief journey.

As you focus on being real and expressing your grief in healthy ways, you will get through this. You will heal, recover, adjust, and grow one step, one moment at a time.

20

WHY DO I FEEL GUILTY WHEN I FEEL BETTER?

This is so hard.

The grief and pain are so deep.

I want to feel better.

**And yet, when I do feel better for
a little while, I feel guilty.**

What's up with that?

The loss of someone we care about feels awful. We're relational creatures who struggle with separation and death. Being apart from those we love runs against the grain of our hearts.

After we've been on the grief journey for a while, most of us long to feel better and to get some relief from all the heaviness. When we do get a grief break and experience some pleasantness for a bit, many of us feel guilty.

How can we feel better, even for a little while? Our friend or loved one is no longer here. There's nothing good in that! We should be miserable, all the time.

When the grief lightens for a bit, perhaps we feel like we're forgetting our loved one or friend. Maybe we're afraid we're leaving them behind or not honoring them as we should.

We will never forget them, but that doesn't mean they must be on our minds every single moment.

We will never stop loving them, but that doesn't mean that we will never do anything again except mourn their death.

We will never leave them behind because they have become a part of us. Their impact and influence in our lives is huge. They live on through us.

As we lean forward into the grief journey, the grief will change over time. As we process and express what's happening inside us in healthy ways, we will experience more breaks in the grief cloud that surrounds us. We will feel better, here and there. The loss will settle into our hearts in new ways. The one we lost will take their new place in our lives.

If you feel guilty when you feel better, rest assured that this is natural and common. It doesn't mean that feeling better is wrong. It means that things are changing again.

When you feel better, embrace that moment as a gift - a grief break and also a promise of the healing still ahead. If guilt comes knocking, acknowledge its presence and then release it as best you can.

Affirmation:

**When I have a good day, I'll welcome it as
a gift and receive it gladly. If guilt comes, I
will acknowledge it and then release it.**

Suggestions:

Here are some things to consider if you feel guilty when you feel better.

- Acknowledge the guilt. Identify the thoughts behind it. "I feel guilty because I am thinking..." Release these thoughts and the guilt as best you can. Whenever guilt surfaces, A.I.R. it out (acknowledge, identify, release). The more you do this, the more guilt will recede into the background over time.

- Consider writing about the guilt you feel. Get it down on paper or on a computer screen, then try reading out loud what you've written. This slows down your mind and heart and helps "get the grief out" in a constructive way.

- Make a list of things you're thankful for. As you begin to write, chances are more and more things and people will come to mind. Keep this list. Look at it from time to time. Perhaps post it in a place where you will see it regularly.

As you process your grief in healthy ways, you'll be better able to see and welcome the goodness in your daily life.

21

HOW DO I STOP THIS TERRIBLE ACHE IN MY HEART?

At first, my heart was shattered.

I didn't know how to feel. I was stunned.

Then came the pain.

The intensity shocked me.

Now I live with this pain - this chronic aching.

How do I stop this terrible ache in my heart?

At first, we're shocked and stunned.

When we come to, we shake our heads in denial. "No. This cannot be happening. It's not true."

When the ugly reality sinks in, the pain begins to surface. It can be so intense we wonder if it might kill us.

We begin to live with this new pain. It invades every nook and cranny of our lives. Over time, a chronic ache settles over us.

This heartache can be so immense that it becomes hard to breathe emotionally. All of life seems to be about our loss. Grief encompasses everything in our world.

Finally, our soul cries out: "When will this pain end? How do I stop this terrible heartache?"

You can't stop this heartache. The ache is there for a good reason. You have a heart. Your heart has been hit hard by loss. Your heart is hurting.

This heartache is real. It must be accepted as it is. Your heartache honors the one you lost. The ache proclaims your love and affection.

As you accept this heartache - and yourself as you are at present - something begins to happen over time. The ache is still there, but it changes. As you express this ache through talking, writing, or art, you're giving this great internal wound some much-needed air.

As you connect and share with safe, trustworthy people who take your heartache seriously, they provide some of the salve your wound needs.

Accept where you are. Process what's happening inside you. Connect with healthy people. Share with those you trust. These things combined lead to healing.

Again, you will heal, but you will never be the same. Let your heartache lead you to love and live more fully than ever.

Affirmation:

My heartache honors my loved one and shouts my love for them. I'll accept this heartache, process it well, and stay connected to safe, loving people.

Suggestions:

Deep heartache is natural and to be expected during a season of heavy loss. Here are a few tips on managing this internal pain.

- Embrace the heartache. It honors the one you lost. Your heart is saying, "I love you." Give yourself permission to hurt and to grieve.

- Consider using T.W.A. (talk it out, write it out, art it out) to express and process what's happening inside you. Talk about your heartache. Describe it. Express whatever comes to mind. Be as specific as possible. Open the spillways of your grief reservoir. For a detailed explanation on T.W.A., see the end of chapter 10.

- Connect with someone you trust who will take your heartache seriously. Let them know you need to express some things and that you need them to just listen. As others accept you where you are, you'll be better able to accept yourself amid all the tumult and upheaval of this loss.

Someone special to you is missing. Embracing and expressing your heartache will be important in your grief process.

"Should you shield the valleys from the windstorms, you would never see the beauty of their canyons."

—Elizabeth Kubler-Ross

PART TWO:

THE MENTAL CHALLENGES

"My mind can't settle.
My brain is on overload.
I can barely put two thoughts together."
-Brian

22

WHY CAN'T MY MIND REST?

My mind never sleeps.

My thoughts bounce about, all over the place.

My mind spins.

Why can't my mind rest?

What can I do to calm my restless mind?

Loss not only hits our hearts. It also greatly impacts our minds.

When news of the loss arrives, our minds freeze. After a short paralysis, they shift into high gear. We wonder about this and that. Questions surface from every corner of our brains. Our thoughts rise and gather, forming themselves into an ongoing orbit. As time goes on, other thoughts are added to this swirling, circling mass in our brains.

Our minds are trying to make sense of things. Yet so much of our loss doesn't make sense. Though the death might be understood rationally, our minds still work on it, picking apart every possible detail and piece of evidence.

We want to know everything. What happened? Why? How? Who was present? Did our friend or loved one say anything? How did they react? What was it all like?

If we were there, we know some of the answers, so our restless minds target other issues. What led up to this? Who else interacted with them recently? What were their final days like, and how did they spend their time?

Our churning brains don't stop there. We wonder about all the intangibles. Did they have peace in their heart? Did they have any unfinished business with anyone? What was in their mind and heart? Did they think about us? How did they really feel about us, deep down?

The questions go on, and on, and on.

Some of these questions will be answered. Some never will. We must learn to live with both - the answers we find and the silent unknowns that remain.

Has your mind been spinning since the death of your loved one or friend? Do you find yourself wondering about some things? Is your mind restless at times, or perhaps all the time?

If so, you're experiencing a mental spinning that is natural and common on this grief journey.

Accept the fact that your mind will be restless for a while. Remember that acceptance of what is empowers you to take the next step in your grief journey, whatever that might happen to be.

Affirmation:

I will accept myself in the moment, bouncing thoughts and all. Over time, I will make sense of what I can and try and release the rest.

Suggestions:

Mental spinning is common in the grief process. Here are some tips to help manage these mental challenges.

- Practice deep breathing (see chapter five for a detailed explanation). This important grief skill will have more impact over time than you can imagine. If you're willing to make it a habit by practicing it several times a day, the benefits will add up and spread over your entire grief process.

- Write down your thoughts and wonderings. This automatically slows your mind down and helps you focus. Many times, just "getting it out" will bring some relief. If you can't write them down for some reason, talk out loud. Putting your thoughts into words and hearing yourself saying them can be powerful.

- As you record your spinning thoughts, notice if there are patterns to the things that seem to be troubling to you. We all have certain things that disturb us more than others.

- Whenever you find your mind spinning, try to take a few minutes to "get it out" somehow. Talk out loud or jot these thoughts down. The more you do this, the better able you will be to process these thoughts when they come.

When you sense your mind spinning, accept yourself in the moment and do what you can to express what you're thinking. Your thoughts matter.

23

WHY CAN'T I THINK STRAIGHT?

My brain is foggy.

My head is heavy.

My thoughts are hazy.

I can't think straight.

What's wrong with me?

───────────────

At some point in the grief journey, many grievers experience some brain fog.

Our brains feel tired. Our thinking is hazy. Our minds are anything but sharp. Our mental processes feel slow or even lethargic. Our heads feel heavy, like some unseen weight is pulling our foreheads down toward the ground.

The heaviness of grief is taking its toll on our minds.

After a close loss, one of the results of our minds not being able to rest is mental fatigue. Our brains get tired. Our circling, cycling thoughts have worn us out.

If we're used to performing at a high level mentally, this can be a rude shock. We can wonder what's happening. We might even have thoughts that perhaps some insidious disease or serious infection is at work.

In most cases, the heavy head, hazy thinking, and brain fatigue adds up to a grief brain fog that is natural and common during a season of loss.

If you're concerned that some health issue might be developing, it's always a good idea to get checked out. When we're grieving, we tend to need more reassurance than normal. You don't need any extra burdens of uncertainty.

If you find yourself mentally fatigued and having trouble putting focused thoughts together, give yourself a break. You're grieving. Try to accept this new state as it is for what it is - a temporary phase on your grief journey. As you continue to process your grief in healthy ways, your mental clarity will most likely slowly return over time.

The loss of your friend or loved one is literally messing with your mind. This is natural and common in grief.

Affirmation:

If I experience some brain fog, I'll remind myself that this is natural and common in the grief journey. I will heal and bounce back over time.

Suggestions:

Here are some tips for handling the mental fatigue that often accompanies a close loss.

- Give yourself time and space. Resist the temptation to push yourself as if nothing has happened. Too much activity can push our grief even further inside. Allow yourself some margin to just be. Accept yourself in the moment.

- Express how you're feeling. Consider using T.W.A. (talk it out, write it out, art it out) to process the brain fog when it comes. See the end of chapter 10 for an explanation of T.W.A.

- Here are a few writing prompts that might help. "Some signs I'm mentally fatigued are..." "When it comes to my current mental state, I'm concerned that..." "I can tell grief is affecting my mind by..."

- Consider connecting with someone you trust. Share what you're feeling and thinking. If you're concerned, seek some reassurance. If you consult a physician, make sure they know you're going through a season of loss and grief.

Brain fog is frustrating. Tell yourself, "This is part of grief."

24

WHAT HAPPENED TO MY FOCUS AND CONCENTRATION?

My thoughts are scattered.

I get distracted so easily.

I can't focus or concentrate like I used to.

I'm worried and frightened about this.

Is something wrong with me?

When loss comes, our minds are stunned and shaken. Our ability to focus and concentrate is affected.

Grief is taking up more and more of our internal real estate. Our minds spin. Our thoughts are scattered and fragmented. We're desperately searching for answers and trying to make sense of this terrible loss.

All the change we're dealing with begins to take its toll. We get tired, fatigued, exhausted. Our circuits get overloaded and our mental energies get squeezed.

No wonder we have trouble focusing. Concentration now takes supreme effort. We wear out quickly. Our former mental stamina seems to have disappeared.

We wonder what's happening. We're not ourselves. We can't perform like we used to. Our work suffers. Simply put, we have less to give right now.

If you're experiencing lapses in focus and concentration, take heart. Decreased mental capacity is natural and common among those on the grief journey.

Rest and good sleep are always important. They are crucial during seasons of loss and stress. Many experience sleep disturbances as well, which only add to the overall difficulty of the grief process.

Rest as you can. Be aware of your limitations. Know that this current downturn in focus and concentration is most likely grief-related and temporary. As you walk this grief road and process what's happening inside you in healthy ways, over time you'll begin to notice your mental energies returning.

Trying harder is not the answer. Accepting yourself and these temporary limitations is important. Once you accept what is, you can begin to work with it.

Take the long view. This concentration handicap is not forever. You're grieving. You are expressing your love for the one who is no longer here. They were and are important to you. Their departure naturally affects your present life in many, many ways.

Decreased ability to focus and concentrate is a natural and common part of the grief process.

Affirmation:

When I can't focus or concentrate like I used to, I'll accept myself and this temporary limitation as part of the grief process. I'll be patient with myself through this.

Suggestions:

When hit by loss, our ability to concentrate is usually affected. Here are some tips for managing this challenge.

- Make lists. Keep a calendar. Having a priority to-do list each day can be helpful. A simple list and up-to-date calendar can release our minds from having to capture and remember everything.

- As you make your daily to-do list, ask yourself, "What's realistic for me right now? What's most important today?" List things in priority order. Keep the list as short as possible. Tackle the top priority on your list. If you finish that, move on to number two. You might even want to take a break after each item is accomplished. Be thankful for each step taken.

- Set yourself up for healing by practicing good self-care. Good nutrition, hydration, rest, and exercise all play an important role in this. For more information on taking good care of yourself during this time, see the end of chapter 38.

- Take your heart and grief seriously. Do a few things well. Let the rest go. In the end, only a few things really matter.

Don't expect to remember everything. An up-to-date calendar and a short, realistic priority list can be important tools in your daily routine.

25

WHAT'S HAPPENING TO MY MEMORY?
AM I LOSING MY MIND?

I'm forgetting things - more than usual.

I forget where I put things, where I'm going, and what I'm supposed to be doing.

I forget appointments. I can't remember what happened an hour ago.

What's happening to my memory?

Am I losing my mind?

In a world where we're on the alert for dementia-related diseases, sudden increased forgetfulness can be terrifying. Many grieving hearts tussle with disturbing memory issues during times of loss.

We forget what day it is. We can't remember where we put our keys, what we're supposed to do next, and what happened yesterday (or 30 minutes ago). We can't recall people's names. We have trouble finding the right words in conversation.

This can be disturbing enough that we can wonder if we're losing our minds.

The grief process is mentally taxing. As grief takes up more of our internal space, our mental capacity naturally gets squeezed. Memory issues are a common result.

If you're experiencing increased forgetfulness, chances are it's related to the heavy loss you're enduring. Breathe deeply. Know that grief is putting a drain on your mental faculties. Be patient with yourself.

What can make this more challenging is that others may notice this difference and not be patient or accepting about it. They're used to you being a certain way and performing at a certain level. Instead of being compassionate, they can be quick to judge and express their displeasure.

Relationships with friends, family, and coworkers can be sources of great stress when we're grieving. We'll talk much more about this and how to handle it in Part Five of this book (Chapters 49-61).

If you're concerned about your mental state, please seek the input of a medical or mental health professional. Expert opinions can supply some of the reassurance you need during this time of upheaval.

Increased forgetfulness and memory issues are natural and common for those on the grief journey.

Affirmation:

If I experience increased forgetfulness, I'll remember that this is common in grief. I'll be patient with myself and trust this will improve over time.

Suggestions:

- As mentioned in the previous chapter, making a short, realistic priority list for each day can be helpful. An up-to-date calendar can relieve a lot of stress.

- In addition to a short, daily priority list, many find it helpful to also keep a master to-do list. This list contains things that you sense need to be addressed, but not today. Each morning, you can refer to this list in case something there needs to be one of your priorities for that day.

- Take a note pad or something similar with you wherever you go. As something comes to mind that you want to remember, jot it down. Don't burden yourself with having to remember it. When you get home, add your notes to your master list.

- At the end of each day, take a little time to breathe deeply and give thanks for that day. Be grateful for anything that was accomplished. Release frustrations and disappointments. Find the good in the day.

Life is lived one day at a time. Take things one step at a time. Do what you can to release the disappointments and frustrations along the way.

26

ARE MENTAL BLANK-OUTS NORMAL IN GRIEF?

I'm noticing I blank out sometimes.

I zone out.

I find myself staring at the walls.

It doesn't last long, but it's weird.

**Are these mental blackouts normal?
Should I be concerned?**

Zoning out is a common indicator of fatigue and exhaustion. Adjusting to all the changes a close loss brings is terribly draining.

Earlier we talked about how our "feelers" can shut down when our emotional circuits get overloaded. In the same way, our mental circuitry can get overwhelmed and cause a temporary mental "blank-out."

We're having dinner with a friend and zone out right in the middle of the conversation. We blink and realize we have no idea what they just said.

We're driving to an appointment 20 minutes away. We arrive there and realize we haven't seen anything along the way and have no recollection of the trip.

We're watching a movie and realize we're clueless about what's happening on the screen.

We're working on something and then find ourselves staring blankly at the wall. Minutes have gone by, but we have no sense of the passing of time.

Though these minor blips can be disturbing, they are typically not concerning or dangerous. During these brief mental power outages, our minds shift into "energy saver" mode. We're taking a mental break.

In grief, we can get overly concerned about things that are different and out of the ordinary for us. We're immersed in massive change already, so anything unexpected that is beyond our control becomes disturbing and potentially frightening.

These are not blackouts in the sense that we lose consciousness. We're conscious, but we're not fully aware. We're taking a brain break while awake.

Some athletes experience this regularly. During exercise involving repetitive movements like running or swimming, the mind can go on autopilot. The athlete is "thinking" during this time (their brain is not dormant), but if you ask them afterward what they were thinking about while working out, they may give you a blank look and say, "I don't know. Nothing, I guess."

This is another reason why working out is healthy. It allows our minds to rest.

If you find yourself zoning out at times, please know that many other grieving hearts experience this.

The grieving mind needs rest. Sometimes, it will blip out on its own. Our brains need breaks from the relentless pressure of all the changes a loss can bring.

Affirmation:

If I find myself zoning out at times, I'll remember that this is common for those on this grief journey. I'll breathe deeply and accept myself as I am in the moment.

Suggestions:

Grief "zone-outs" can be disconcerting. When this happens, here are some things to consider:

- Process what you're experiencing. Write down what you're feeling and thinking. What are you concerned about? What frustrates you? What fears seem to lurk beneath the surface? Getting these things out of your heart and mind and down on paper can be relieving.

- If you're concerned about your health, consider touching base with your physician or a grief professional. Make sure your physician is aware of your loss. Consulting an expert can be reassuring and comforting.

- Reach out to someone you trust who knows grief well. Share with them your concerns. Get their perspective.

Give yourself permission to zone out at times. Your mind needs breaks from the constant grind of grief.

27

HOW DO I DEAL WITH TRAUMATIC MENTAL IMAGES?

I'm plagued by what I saw.

The pictures in my brain will not go away.

I add to them other things that I have imagined.

These images haunt me.

How do I deal with this?

How do I get rid of the pictures in my mind?

One terrible truth in life is that we can't un-see something.

Visual images lodge themselves in our minds. If we witness something traumatic, like the suffering and death of someone important to us, that image sears a pathway in our brains. Our minds tend to go there repeatedly.

Traumatic mental images are a huge part of post-traumatic stress. Our hearts, minds, bodies, and souls have witnessed a shocking event. We're hit on every level of our being.

Many times, we add to what we've seen by creating scenes of what we imagine occurred. Even if we didn't witness the traumatic event, we create pictures in our minds of what it might have been like. We contemplate what our friend or loved one might have felt - emotionally and physically. Our imaginary images can be haunting as well.

Post-traumatic stress like this can be debilitating. Flashbacks are often unnerving and terrifying. It's like we're right back there reliving the horrors all over again. Our anxiety can go through the roof. Panic attacks can become commonplace.

If you witnessed the death of your loved one or friend, please be kind to yourself. Experiencing post-traumatic stress is common in such cases. This is painful, disorienting, and extremely challenging.

Disturbing mental images need to be proactively processed. It's hard for us to do that by ourselves. We need other people to help us. We need safe people, good listeners, and compassionate and competent guides to walk with us in this.

If you're dealing with painful mental images or post-traumatic stress, please consider seeking expert help and assistance from a mental health professional who is well-acquainted with such things.

Is it possible to recover and heal from such things? Yes. That may be hard to imagine right now, but you are not alone in experiencing severe trauma. Many have walked this path, sought and received what they needed, and learned to manage this deep pain and begin to use it to heal and grow.

Struggling with traumatic mental images is natural and common for those who have witnessed disturbing scenes. We can't un-see something, but with help we can begin to deal with what we've seen in healthy ways that lead to recovery and healing.

Affirmation:

I'll need help to deal well with any disturbing, traumatic images. I'll reach out, find the help I need, and learn to deal with this pain in a way that leads to healing.

Suggestions:

If you're experiencing disturbing, repetitive mental images, here are some things to remember and consider.

- You can't un-see something. Traumatic images automatically burn themselves into our brains. These mental pictures tend to stay with us.

- These images must be talked about, shared, and processed. When we keep them to ourselves, we only end up giving the trauma more power and influence.

- Consider seeking professional expert assistance. Your heart is worth this. Look for someone with experience in guiding wounded hearts through post-traumatic stress. You want to find ways to take care of yourself, heal, and grow. This honors your loved one and empowers you to have healthier relationships with others.

- Please know that this internalized trauma does not simply go away on its own. The passing of time will not chase it away. We heal when we take our hearts seriously and process what's happening inside us.

Be kind to yourself. Be patient with yourself. This is hard. Healing takes time.

28

HOW DO I HANDLE
LACK OF CLOSURE?

I didn't get to say goodbye.

**I didn't get to hold their hand
and look into their eyes.**

**I didn't get to tell them all they meant to me, to
ask forgiveness, or to even say, "I love you."**

This is awful. It all feels so unfinished.

It's like I'm in limbo with no closure.

What can I do?

Many of us didn't get to say goodbye.

Perhaps we weren't with our loved ones when they died. We didn't get a chance to connect with them and interact. We didn't have an opportunity to ask questions and say what we wanted and needed to say.

Many times, death comes unexpectedly. Life can depart suddenly and without warning. The shock can be immense. We shake our heads. Our hearts scream, "No!"

Other times, we're aware that our loved one or friend is dying, but circumstances keep us from being present or communicating meaningfully with them. The coronavirus pandemic, for example, thrust many of us into unbelievable situations of separation and isolation.

When we don't get these precious final moments with those we love and care about, we feel robbed. We can feel stunned and paralyzed.

When the shock fades, we're often left with a profound sense of emptiness. Everything feels unfinished.

Lack of closure is disturbing and frustrating. Not being able to be present or communicate meaningfully with our friend or loved one only adds to our sadness and anger. In many cases, not being able to properly say goodbye can vastly add to the challenge of our grief journey.

Were you able to be with your loved one when they died? Were you able to communicate meaningfully to them or with them?

Did you get to say what you needed to? Did you get to say goodbye in the way you would have liked?

If you didn't, please know that there are many of us struggling with a lack of closure. You are not alone in this.

There is a sense in which all of us are dealing with not being able to say goodbye the way we wanted to. None of us had a perfect scenario. None of us did all that we wanted to do or said all we wanted and needed to say. We all feel "unfinished" in some way.

Now we must find our own closure somehow. We must make our own opportunities to say goodbye, perhaps long after a death. Though this can be challenging, it can be done.

Saying goodbye is hard and painful. Saying goodbye meaningfully can also be good and healing. Finding a sense of closure is important.

Be kind to yourself in this. Set your mind to move from frustration with how things were to what you can do now to seek a healthy sense of closure. Though that might be hard to imagine, focus on taking the next step in that direction.

Affirmation:

Though I didn't get the closure I would have wanted, I will do what I can now to say goodbye in healthy ways over time.

Suggestions:

If you didn't get a chance to say goodbye in the way you would have liked, here are a few things to consider:

- Though difficult, try to accept things as they were. Acceptance is key to recovery, healing, and adjustment. Acceptance of what was enables you to take the next step in creating your own sense of closure about what happened and how.

- What do you wish you could have said to your loved one? What would you have wanted those final hours and moments to have been like? Take a few moments and write about this. Express your heart.

- Consider writing a letter to your loved one, saying what you wished you could have said. Express your love. Ask forgiveness, if necessary. Be open, real, and honest.

- If you can, imagine your loved one being with you. Read your letter to them. Let yourself hear your own voice saying what you wanted and needed to say.

- Repeat the above process as you want and need to.

How we deal with lack of closure is important. Find ways to express your love and find some of the closure you need. This is hard and can be intense, but it can also be incredibly good and healing.

29

ARE PAST LOSSES COMPLICATING MY GRIEF?

This loss has brought up all the others.

**I keep thinking about the other
people I've lost along the way.**

**The pain is resurfacing. And now
I have this new pain too.**

What do I do with all this?

Are past losses making this loss harder?

Our grief is never just about one loss. Each new loss tends to remind us of past losses. Past pain comes visiting again.

Imagine for a moment that you were given a large suitcase when you were born. As you lived and grew, experiences were loaded into your suitcase. Sadly, negative experiences and losses can often end up being larger and heavier than positive experiences. When we're young, we don't have any idea how to process loss, so we end up having to carry it around with us wherever we go.

As we grow, we experience more losses along the way. To some degree, each successive loss triggers the pain of past losses. If we don't learn how to process and deal with these losses well, more weight gets added to our suitcase. Over time, we can begin to stagger under the sheer weight of all that has been heaped upon us.

We get used to carrying this weight, not knowing that those unprocessed losses have most likely created unhealthy patterns of thinking and living along the way. If we don't begin to process these losses, we can find ourselves suddenly immobilized. We can no longer lift the massive weight upon us. We fall and stagger. We're worn out. All our coping mechanisms fail. We can feel lost, helpless, and undone.

We can feel like hope has disappeared. The reality is that hope is always there, but in heavy grief we often don't have eyes to perceive it. Our eyes are focused on our losses.

Yes, past losses can complicate our current situation and our grief process. However, please know this: No one is beyond repair. Anyone can heal. Anyone can grow - including you.

If past losses are an issue, the first thing we need to do is to be willing to open our life suitcase. We need to consider what's back there - disappointments, rejections, betrayals, abuse, abandonments, estrangements, deaths - and begin to unpack our suitcase a bit. Most likely we will need help to do this well.

If your life suitcase is heavy, consider working through the Personal History of Loss at the end of this chapter. Then consider sharing some or all of that with someone safe and trustworthy. Professional expert help can be extremely valuable here. Mental health professionals who know grief well can be invaluable partners to assist you in unpacking the heavier items in your life suitcase.

We all have past losses. Past pain can become present again with each new loss. Dealing with past losses as well as the present loss is important in the recovery, healing, and growth process.

Affirmation:

My past losses may be contributing to my current pain and grief. I'll find healthy ways to process and heal from the past as well as the present.

A PERSONAL HISTORY OF LOSS

We all have storage boxes in our brains. We tend to force-fully shut and lock the boxes that contain painful, trau-matic experiences. Unfortunately, these things will not be ignored. Our padlocked boxes will fester, corrode, and eventually leak out into our lives. What we don't address and process will affect our health, relationships, and qual-ity of life.

Take a moment and breathe deeply.

Think back to early childhood. Begin listing the losses that come to mind, working from the past to the present day.

Birth to 10 years of age:

_____

_____

_____

11-20 years of age:

_____

_____

_____

21-30 years of age:

_____

_____

_____

31-40 years of age:

_____

_____

_____

41-50 years of age:

_____

_____

_____

After 50 years of age:

_____

_____

_____

Go back through these losses. Put a star or an asterisk beside any that feel painful even today.

Your personal history of loss, especially those experiences marked with a star or asterisk, can form the basis of your sharing and discussion with a safe person or grief professional. Working through and processing these things is somewhat like unpacking baggage that you no longer want to carry.

Past pain often visits the present. Healing is hard work, but well worth it. Don't let past pain determine your present or your future.

30

HOW DO I DEAL WITH MULTIPLE LOSSES?

My losses are piling up.

**I've lost so much - including
people - in the recent past.**

**One after another, the losses and
deaths just keep coming.**

I'm overwhelmed. I can't seem to catch my breath.

How do I deal with all these losses at once?

One close loss is more than enough. Many, however, experience multiple losses all at once or over a short period of time.

Dealing with numerous losses on top of each other is challenging and can be complicated. What we would experience with one loss gets compounded. A lot of loss and grief gets quickly dumped into our life suitcase and the sudden weight can be staggering.

When our hearts are hit hard in rapid succession, we reel with the shock and pain. We get overwhelmed easily. We can feel like we're turning in circles and trying desperately to manage what's coming at us. We're processing one loss and then another gets layered on top of it.

This adds up to what's called "cumulative grief." The losses add up to produce an even more challenging grief process.

After a while, we wonder how much more loss we can endure. The feelings can be so intense and overwhelming that we can find ourselves shifting into avoidance mode. We attempt to run from the pain through busyness, denial, impulsive activities, or even substance abuse.

Using alcohol, drugs, or other substances only prolongs and intensifies the grief process. We might think these substances provide some momentary relief, and yet the pain comes crashing in with even greater intensity afterwards. We wake to find these heavy, numerous, and unresolved losses waiting for us.

We heal and grow when we begin to be real about what's happening inside us and deal with things as they are. We have a unique relationship with each person we lose, and so it makes sense that these losses must be grieved and processed individually, one at a time.

In the case of multiple losses, professional grief assistance is often extremely helpful. Throughout life, we need good, experienced mentors to coach us through difficult seasons and circumstances. Processing multiple losses certainly fits that category.

If you're dealing with several losses over a short period of time, please be kind to yourself. Allow yourself to feel the grief - the shock, pain, sorrow, anger, fear, guilt, etc. Give yourself permission to feel whatever is happening at the moment. When we avoid feeling our grief, we end up compounding the stress that we're under, which can end up compromising our emotional, mental, and physical health.

Enduring multiple losses is terribly challenging. We have hearts, and our hearts need space to work through each loss. This grief work is arduous and exhausting, but well worth it.

As we process each loss in healthy ways, over time we begin to sense healing taking place. Our grief begins to feel different. The heaviness lifts a bit. Some sunlight begins to penetrate the storm clouds of loss.

Affirmation:

Enduring multiple losses at once is extremely challenging. Every relationship is unique, so I will process and grieve each loss well, one at a time.

Suggestions:

Being hit by multiple close losses in a short period of time can be traumatic and even debilitating. Cumulative grief is challenging, but can be processed and managed, one step at a time.

- You are unique, and so are your losses. Your grief journey will not be the same as anyone else's. Give yourself permission to feel what's happening inside, in the present moment.

- Consider working through your Personal History of Loss described in the last chapter. Mark those losses that you sense were particularly significant.

- Take these significant losses one at a time. As you think about each loss, express what's happening inside using T.W.A. (Talk It Out, Write It Out, Art It Out). Take your time. See the end of chapter 10 for a description of using T.W.A. for grief processing.

- Consider consulting a mental health or grief professional for input and feedback. Those tussling with multiple losses can really benefit from a knowledgeable, experienced grief travel companion. They can walk with you through these multiple losses, one loss at a time.

Handling multiple losses is a challenge. Find ways to process each loss, one at a time. Be patient with yourself. This takes time.

31

HOW DO I DEAL WITH SELF-HARMING THOUGHTS?

I fear my pain has led me to a dark place.

I'm wondering, "What's the point. Why am I here?"

I can't imagine a world without my loved one, even though I'm living in that world now.

Sometimes I have thoughts of harming myself.

It's like I can feel myself slipping away.

I don't know what to do with this.

Sometimes the pain of life is so great that we can find ourselves in dark places. The grinding pressure of loss can whittle away at our sense of hope. In some cases, the common grief emotions compound together and lead to a sense of apathy, meaninglessness, and despair.

When self-harming thoughts come, it's crucial to reach out and involve someone we trust. This is dangerous territory that we cannot afford to traverse alone.

Isolation is the number one enemy of the grieving heart. The grief process itself can be isolating. Our relationships change. We can feel like no one understands or cares. Loneliness is common in grief, but when we start to isolate from other people and the world in general, we're entering the danger zone.

We're relational creatures. We're wired for connection. This is why loss and death hurt so much. It's also why it's crucial, no matter what our loss, that we stay connected to other people - preferably healthy, safe people - through this process.

We can't afford to pull away and go internal with our pain. We must be real with what's happening inside us and find ways to "get it out" and process it. If we don't, the internal pressure continues to build. The pain begins to gnaw away at our already shattered hearts.

If we're in a dark place, it can seem like hope has departed. The key words here are "seem like." The reality is that hope is always here, but our lenses may be so clouded by grief and pain that we can't see it.

We need to clean our glasses a bit. When things are foggy, that's difficult to do on our own. We need people in our lives. We need some compassionate, listening, loving hearts that will enter our world and walk with us on this winding, uphill path.

If you're having thoughts of harming yourself or of ending your life, please reach out to someone immediately. You are unique in human history and far more important than you realize. We need you.

No matter how dark things seem or how deep the pain, hope is always here.

Affirmation:

If I have thoughts of harming myself, I'll reach out and involve someone else immediately. I choose to believe that hope is here, even if I can't perceive it right now.

Suggestions:

If you're having thoughts of harming yourself or of ending your life, please reach out now. Contact someone you trust. Call the National Suicide Hotline at 800-273-8255 or text 741741.

After you make contact, keep reaching out. Don't slip back into thinking you can handle this alone. None of us can. We're relational by nature. We're all different, but we're in this together.

Keep telling yourself, "There are people out there who will not only walk with me, but who **want** to walk with me." This isn't just wishful thinking. It's true.

Reach out. Keep reaching out. You're more important than you know. We need you.

"Where you used to be,

there is a hole in the world,

which I find myself constantly walking around in the daytime,

and falling in at night."

—Edna St. Vincent Millay

PART THREE:

THE PHYSICAL DISTRESS

"I feel like my body is betraying me.
I have one health issue after another.
There are times when I think my grief might kill me."
-Carol

32

WHY AM I SO TIRED ALL THE TIME?

I'm tired all the time.

I'm drained. I have no energy.

I wake up tired. I work tired. I come home tired. I go to bed tired.

The fatigue is getting to me.

Sometimes I can barely lift my head.

Loss impacts our bodies too. The number one physical symptom grieving hearts experience is fatigue.

Most people underestimate the incredible amount of change that comes with a loss. We lose a person, and then we begin to lose almost everything attached to them - companionship, activities, expectations, hopes, dreams, relationships. etc. This whirlwind of change and the accompanying grief is exhausting.

This grief fatigue is natural and common. Nothing is wrong with us. Our worlds are different now. Trying to process and adjust to it all takes a stunning amount of energy.

We will not be able to do all that we did before this loss. There's not enough of us left to keep up that pace. Life is different. Grief is taking up more of our internal space and energies.

Our work performance will not be what it was. It can't be. We're not going to be on top of our game for a while, and that's okay. Life is not business as usual right now.

Our relationships will be more challenging. We have less energy and focus available to relate well. We might find ourselves easily irritated and frustrated. Our patience with others gets squeezed.

Even when we're not dealing with a loss, we don't do as well when we're tired. Fatigue affects everything. Exhaustion can severely limit what we can do and how.

We might think that rest is the answer. Certainly, giving ourselves space to do a little less and rest a little more is huge. Every little bit of down time can help. Rest is terrifically important. Having said that, however, we need to accept the fact that we're going to be tired, simply because loss and grief are terribly draining.

If you're experiencing fatigue and exhaustion, please know that this is part of the grief journey. Everything can feel like an energy-sucking chore. One grieving heart even said, "I can barely eat. Chewing takes way too much effort."

Breathe deeply. Be kind to yourself. Rest when you can.

Affirmation:

I'll remember that fatigue is common in times of loss. I'll downgrade my expectations of myself, pay attention to my energy level, and take rest seriously.

Suggestions:

Grief fatigue can be frustrating. Here are a few tips to help manage it:

- Practice deep breathing. Schedule it into your day and make it a habit. This is a form of rest. See the end of chapter five for a detailed description of this crucial grief skill.

- Consider downgrading your expectations of yourself. Now is not normal, so your expectations of yourself shouldn't be normal either. Plan on doing less than usual. Doing a few things well, rather than pushing to do more things on an already empty tank, will help rebuild your confidence and sense of purpose.

- Work in shorter intervals. Take frequent rest breaks during the day. Set an alarm on your phone if necessary. This will improve your performance and help keep you sane.

- Consider taking a short nap in the afternoon. Begin by breathing deeply. A brief rest, even if you don't sleep, can help in the long run. We need more breaks than we realize, especially now.

Grief is incredibly draining. Take the fatigue seriously. Give yourself permission to do less and to rest more.

33

WHY AM I HAVING ALL THESE STRANGE PHYSICAL SYMPTOMS?

I'm having headaches and stomach distress.

My muscles are tight. My body aches.

My heartbeat is weird. It skips around and races at times.

I feel lethargic. My body feels heavy.

What's happening? Why am I having all these strange symptoms?

———————————

Almost all of us experience some form of physical distress while grieving. Having new or exacerbated symptoms is common.

Stomach distress, gastrointestinal issues, headaches, muscle and joint pain, palpitations, racing heartbeat, trembling, nausea, dizziness, higher blood pressure, sinus problems, and muscle twitching are not unusual. Grief is a form of stress. It challenges our immune system and increases inflammation which can worsen current health problems or give rise to new ones.

Loss pounds our bodies more than we realize.

On the heels of the death of a friend or loved one, sudden physical issues - either new or exacerbated - get our attention. Having already been dealt a severe blow, we're naturally less resilient than usual. We worry more easily. We're more prone to fear and anxiety. The last thing we need is another unknown coming at us.

If we're concerned about what we're experiencing physically, it's usually best to get it checked out. We can always benefit from a little reassurance when everything seems so upside down. We need to offload all the potential worry and uncertainty we can.

Accepting the fact that we're stressed is the first step. Just knowing that we will most likely experience some physical upset can be helpful. When the symptoms come, then we can decide what to do with them.

Health issues can be disconcerting and even terrifying. Part of a healthy grief journey includes taking our physical health seriously and seeking the help we need along the way.

If new or worsened physical symptoms are part of your grief process so far, please know that this is extremely common. Be kind to yourself. Keep breathing deeply. Rest as you can. Seek expert advice and reassurance when needed.

None of us are invincible. We're human and limited - perhaps more than we realize. Thankfully, now is not forever. As we process our grief in healthy ways, we will heal, adjust, and grow through this.

Affirmation:

Grief is stressful and might affect my health. I'll take this seriously and reach out for assistance and reassurance when I need it.

Suggestions:

Experiencing new or exacerbated physical symptoms can be unnerving and scary. Here are some tips on how to manage this stress.

- Consider keeping a symptom log. Use a calendar and record the symptoms you experience and their severity (with 1 being slight and 10 being the worst possible). You will be able to see any patterns that emerge and know in a semi-objective way whether your symptoms are getting better or worse over time. Your symptom log will be invaluable if you need to talk to a physician about your symptoms.

- Make exercise a priority. Exercise in a way that fits your age and health. Consult your physician before starting an exercise program. Over time, exercise can help you manage your grief stress and potentially reduce some of your troubling symptoms.

- Consider adding some vitamins or immune-boosting supplements. Consult your physician about this. Make sure they know about your loss and any current physical challenges. In times of loss, we can use all the help we can get!

- If you're concerned about your health, please get checked out. You don't need extra worry right now.

Contact your physician. Get the help and reassurance you need.

New or worsening physical symptoms can be distressing. Grief can exact a physical toll.

34

WHY CAN'T I SLEEP LIKE I USED TO?

My sleep patterns are way off.

I go to bed and it takes me forever to get to sleep.

I wake up frequently.

**When the alarm does go off, I
wonder if I've slept at all.**

I never feel rested anymore.

Why can't I just sleep the way I used to?

———————

After a loss, our minds and hearts are always working. We're trying to make sense of this new world we find ourselves in. Sleep disturbances during all this are natural and common.

We have trouble resting. We lay down, but our minds are spinning. We're not doing anything, but our heart rate is up. We have difficulty falling asleep. Once we fall asleep, we can't seem to stay asleep. Even if we get what used to be ample hours of sleep, now we wake up tired and anything but refreshed.

It's been said that sleep deprivation is the most basic form of torture. Over time, sleep disturbances can exact a heavy toll.

When we sleep, we not only rest, but we also heal. Our bodies and systems rejuvenate. During seasons of loss, our system is taxed even more than usual. At the time when restful sleep is even more crucial, our minds, hearts, and bodies don't seem to be cooperating.

In addition, dreams and nightmares can complicate things even further. Some dreams can be wonderful and reassuring, which can be encouraging and even helpful. Other dreams might only increase our longing for our friend or loved one. Nightmares, of course, are disturbing and even traumatizing.

No wonder sleep is often an issue for grieving hearts.

As with other parts of the grieving process, acceptance is the first step to dealing with what is. We take a deep breath and remind ourselves that sleep difficulties are natural and common after a loss. We're adjusting to a myriad of changes and the process is bumpy at best.

Secondly, we focus on grieving in healthy ways. We process our thoughts and emotions and "get the grief out" as best we can. We try to connect with safe, trustworthy people. We guard against isolation and addictive behaviors. As we do these things, some aspects of life begin to settle a bit. Over time, sleep patterns usually even out as well.

In the meantime, doing what we can to calm our minds and bodies becomes important. Deep breathing, relaxation techniques, prayer, and meditation are helpful to many.

If you're experiencing challenging changes in your sleep patterns, rest assured that nothing weird or strange is going on. Sleep disturbances are natural and common for those who are grieving.

Affirmation:

Altered sleep patterns are common for those suffering from a close loss. I'll be kind to myself and do what I can to process my grief and calm my heart and mind over time.

Suggestions:

Sleep disturbances are common in grief. Here are some things to consider.

- Practice deep breathing (see the end of chapter five for more info). As deep breathing becomes a habit, you'll be able to use it more and more to relax and rest.

- As you are winding down for bedtime, consider releasing the day, piece by piece. Take a few minutes and go back through your day from beginning to end. Release each part of the day as you go along - good things, challenging things, painful moments, interactions, events, etc. Breathe deeply as you release your day, bit by bit.

- Consider trying some visualization. Picture yourself in a safe relaxing place. Perhaps it's a special place you've been where you felt safe, secure, and peaceful. Rest in the moment. Try to release the things that come to mind. Try visualization at some time during the day, and then again at night before sleep.

Sleep disturbances are common in grief. Do your best to accept what is and release what you can along the way.

35

WHY DON'T I ENJOY FOOD ANYMORE?

**My eating has become mechanical.
I'm going through the motions.**

My food is tasteless and dull.

My appetite is gone.

Sometimes I have to force myself to eat.

**What's happening to me? Why
don't I enjoy food anymore?**

Heavy grief tends to dull the senses, including our taste buds. After a loss, food doesn't taste the same.

Loss hits us so hard that we can forget to eat. We have little to no appetite. Our eating can become mechanical and lifeless - just one more thing we must do. As a natural consequence, many lose weight during their grief journey.

If we really enjoyed food before, this can be profoundly disturbing. Everything in life seems to have lost its savor, including food.

For others, the stress of loss causes us to eat more. Desperate for comfort, we seek to ease our pain with food.

Even then, however, our eating tends to be mechanical. We rarely really taste or enjoy our food.

The stress of grief is heavy. It affects every part of us, including our desire for and enjoyment of food.

In times of great stress, however, good nutrition and hydration become preeminently important. Our bodies need support to function well during this challenging season.

Eating well is intentional and takes planning and energy that many of us don't have while grieving. This makes managing our nutritional intake even more difficult.

All this adds up to more adjustment and change. Even what and how much we eat is affected. The incredible stress of it all can be overwhelming.

If you're experiencing changes in appetite, nutritional intake, or weight changes, please know that these upheavals are common for most of us on this winding road of grief.

Accept yourself as best you can amid these changes. Practice breathing deeply. Know that as you process your grief in healthy ways, most likely your appetite and enjoyment of food will return over time.

If you're struggling to the point where you can't seem to eat or stop eating, please consider reaching out to a mental health or grief professional for input. Your health is paramount.

Getting good nutrition aids in the grief process more than most of us realize.

Affirmation:

Even though food might have lost its savor, I'll be intentional about good nutrition while grieving. Over time, this can make a huge difference.

Suggestions:

When it comes to food and good nutritional intake during this season of loss, here are a few suggestions to consider:

- Accept what is as best you can. Now is not forever. As you continue to process what's happening inside you, the grief will change over time.

- When you eat, take your time. Focus on eating and try to enjoy your food. For many, this makes a profound difference, and they find themselves tasting and enjoying their meals a bit more over the days and weeks.

- Hydration is huge. Research indicates that 75% of us are walking around dehydrated. Getting enough water and electrolytes can make a massive difference in your overall wellness. Consult a health professional for input.

- Consider sharing any food struggles with at least one safe, trustworthy person. Someone else knowing what you're going through can be relieving and comforting. Those around you can also be an encouragement as you navigate this weird food phase.

- If you're struggling with food issues and appetite, you might want to involve your physician or an experienced medical professional. Expert advice and input can make all the difference.

Again, don't attempt to manage all this alone. Others need to be aware of what's happening in your life. This helps both you and them.

36

HOW DID I BECOME SO ACCIDENT PRONE?

I think I'm falling apart.

I stumble and fall.

I trip over my own two feet.

I bump into walls, corners, and people.

I can't seem to park the car straight anymore.

How did I become so accident-prone?

Grief affects our minds and our bodies. Many find themselves having coordination issues of some kind. We can become rather accident-prone.

We cut ourselves while chopping vegetables. We raise up and whack our head against the cabinet door we forgot to close. We spin around too quickly, our legs get tangled, and down we go. We turn and bump into a wall. We drop things more often. We go to sit down and almost miss the chair. We stumble more while walking. Driving becomes more challenging.

Our depth perception is off. Our brains and bodies don't seem to be communicating as well. We're not ourselves at present.

These changes can be frustrating and disturbing. We might wonder about our health. "What's wrong? Do I have a brain tumor or something?" one grieving heart said.

Accidents can be frightening. Some mishaps can be dangerous. We need to be aware of possible coordination issues and be even more careful than before. As with every other area of life, we need to adjust for the incredible stress that loss brings.

If you're having more accidents, remember that this is natural and common for those enduring a season of loss. Continue doing what you can to express the grief inside in proactive healthy ways. Most of these coordination challenges will resolve themselves over time.

Sometimes, however, we need expert reassurance that we're okay physically. Many consult their physician just to make sure there is nothing of concern that needs to be addressed. Medical professionals can also give good advice for how to maneuver better through this stress-laden season.

Grief stress is more pervasive than we realize. It leaves nothing untouched in our lives. Being kind to ourselves and patient with ourselves is crucial. Exercising an extra bit of caution during this accident-prone time is wise.

Affirmation:

**Being more accident prone while griev-
ing is common. I'll exercise a bit
more caution during this time.**

Suggestions:

If you find yourself being a little less coordinated and a bit more accident-prone, here are a few things to consider:

- Remind yourself to be a bit more cautious than usual. Slow down a little. Take extra precautions when engaged in activities like driving, cooking, operating machinery, working with sharp objects, using ladders, etc.

- Don't be in a hurry. Your system is being squeezed by grief. Intentionally take your time and slow down a bit. A hurried sense of urgency can set you up for a fall - literally. "Slow but sure" can be a good strategy while grieving.

- Keep processing your grief in healthy ways. "Get the grief out" proactively whenever you can. Talk it out. Write it out. Use art. As you express what's happening inside you, it can ease the intensity and physical impact of your grief.

- If coordination issues persist, please consult a physician. Make sure you let them know about your recent loss and any new or worsening physical symptoms you've been experiencing.

Take your time. Slow it down a little. Be a bit more cautious than usual. You don't need an accident or injury right now.

37

HOW DO I HANDLE PANIC ATTACKS?

I'm having panic attacks now.

They're awful and terrifying.

Sometimes, I feel like I'm dying.

I'm a disaster. I feel so out of control.

What can I do?

Panic attacks are indeed terrifying. Sadly, they tend to be common in the grief journey.

Sometimes we know what the trigger is. We see something and begin thinking about this or that. We get anxious. The anxiety takes off. We feel the panic coming. Soon, we're hyperventilating, light-headed, and terror-stricken.

Other times, we can't identify a trigger at all. We seem to be fine, doing daily life and minding our own business. Anxiety descends on us seemingly out of nowhere. Panic ensues and hijacks us.

Panic attacks can be debilitating.

The insidious thing about panic attacks is that they are so awful that we begin fearing the next one before it arrives. Over time, that anticipatory anxiety can lead to another panic attack.

Though panic attacks are not uncommon for grieving hearts, they are not something we should attempt to manage on our own. Most of us are embarrassed by these sudden assaults of terror, which can lead us to isolate a bit. However, now is the very time when we need to be reaching out.

Though we don't tend to share this struggle with others, it is wise and helpful to involve some trustworthy, safe people in this battle with us. We need the support and understanding of others. They can give invaluable input and bring perspective.

To manage panic attacks well, however, most need some professional guidance. Licensed counselors and grief professionals can provide the listening ears, compassionate acceptance, and expert assistance we need to navigate these fear-laced upheavals. These professionals, along with our physician, can help determine whether medication or supplements might be helpful.

The expert help we need may be costly at times. Investing heavily in our own recovery, healing, and wellness is a huge priority. One of the best gifts we can give to ourselves and those around us is to be as healthy as possible. Taking care of ourselves is also a powerful way to honor those we've lost.

If you find yourself having panic attacks, please take your heart seriously and reach out to someone who can walk with you through this. Don't try to do this alone. We need each other.

Affirmation:

If I experience panic attacks, I'll be careful not to isolate, but instead reach out for the assistance I need to handle these attacks in healthy ways.

Suggestions:

If you find yourself having anxiety or panic attacks, please consider the following.

- Remember that you are far from alone. Many experience panic attacks as part of their grief journey.

- Practice deep breathing and make it a habit (see the end of chapter five). This simple skill can make a big difference. While panic is sending emergency fight-or-flight messages to your brain, deep breathing sends the message, "Things are not as bad as panic says. I am not in danger. This will pass."

- When a panic attacks comes, try accepting what is. "I'm feeling panicky. I'll accept this panic as part of my grief process." I know that might sound scary or even crazy, but the reality is that once you accept what's happening in the moment, in most cases the panic actually begins to dissipate.

- Is there a counselor or grief professional you can talk with about panic attacks? If you don't know anyone personally, whom can you talk to for some guidance or a recommendation? Getting some expert input can be invaluable in dealing with tough issues like this.

- Do you have a physician that you trust? Would you be willing to make a call or make an appointment to talk about panic attacks with them? Make sure you tell them about your loss and your grief process so far.

Panic attacks can be terrifying. Breathe deeply. Try to accept what is in the moment. Tell yourself, "I will get through this. This will pass."

38

CAN GRIEF MAKE ME SICK?

My body is betraying me.

I'm sick all the time.

I run into one health issue after another.

I hardly ever feel good anymore.

Is grief making me sick?

––––––––––––

The simple answer is, "Yes. Loss and the resulting grief can affect us physically to the point of illness."

Loss is extremely stressful. Grief has no time limit, which means that the particular stress of losing someone we love and care about is ongoing. Stress is a grinding influence. The longer the intensity lasts, the more the pressure wears on our hearts, minds, and bodies.

We've also said before that stress tends to suppress and even erode the immune system. We can become more susceptible to colds, flus, and other illnesses.

The stress of our loss, combined with all the other, usual stresses of life, can potentially produce health issues over time. Therefore, doing what we can to offload what stress we can is crucial.

We need to remember that now is not business as usual. Life is different. We are different. We're slogging through innumerable changes and attempting to manage unruly thoughts and emotions. This is draining and exhausting. Learning to manage anxiety and release fear and worry is important.

Simply put, anything healthy we can do to reduce our stress load is helpful. We need relief. We need space and time. We can only deal well with so much at one time.

Doing what we can to "get the grief out" and process it in healthy ways aids in reducing our stress load, which in turn benefits our physical health and mental wellness. Making self-care a priority can be one of the best things we can do during a season of heavy loss (more info about self-care in the next chapter).

Enduring grief stress over an extended period often leads to some health struggles for those on the grief journey. If you're having new or exacerbated health issues and more frequent illnesses, you're not alone or unusual. Be kind to yourself and do what you can to process your grief well.

Affirmation:

Knowing that grief can lead to stress-related health issues, I'll do what I can to process this loss well, stay connected to some safe people, and guard my health.

Suggestions:

Here's a quick summary of tips to consider if you think you're experiencing grief stress related illnesses or health issues:

- Accept where you are at present. Acceptance helps empower you to respond to what's happening rather than remain stuck in reaction mode.

- Contact your physician and let them know what's happening in your life and what you're experiencing.

- Continue to process your grief in healthy ways. "Get it out" by using T.W.A. (see the end of chapter 10 for more info). Connect with safe, trustworthy people. Seek expert opinions and advice from mental health and grief professionals as needed along the way.

- Examine your expectations of yourself at present. Consider making a personal expectation list. How realistic are your expectations? Most likely, you need to expect a little less of yourself during this time.

Intense grief can be physically grinding. Put self-care high on your priority list. More on this in the next chapter.

39

HOW DO I TAKE CARE OF MYSELF WHILE GRIEVING?

I'm used to pushing it.

I take care of business. I take care of people.

I'm used to being independent and in charge.

Now I'm grieving and overloaded. I feel myself cratering.

How do I care for myself during all this?

We pride ourselves on being competent and independent. We work hard, achieve, and provide. We nurture and take care of others. If we have enough margin, we manage to pursue what personal wellness we can.

Then our lives are upended by a close loss. Our worlds are altered. Our routine as we knew it disappears. Everything begins to change, including us. Our margin - all that time and space we used for personal wellness and fun - gets gobbled up by grief.

In times of loss, self-care often takes a back seat to, well, everything else. We drag ourselves out of bed in the morning and try to follow through with our responsibilities.

We focus our diminishing energies on the stuff we think we "have to do." Self-care often falls into the "optional" category.

If we're going to grieve in healthy ways, live well, love those around us, and honor those we've lost, we must move self-care from the back of our minds to the top of our agenda.

What does good self-care while grieving look like?

Here are some of the obvious facets of self-care, many of which have been mentioned in previous chapters:

- Giving ourselves permission to hurt and to grieve.

- Practicing healthy ways to process the grief inside us.

- Connecting with safe, trustworthy people who are helpful to us.

- Guarding our hearts against negative, toxic, and unhelpful influences.

- Intentionally protecting our health through good nutrition, hydration, and rest.

- Embracing the importance of exercise and healthy physical activity.

- Seeking expert assistance when needed from medical, mental health, and grief professionals.

- Connecting with mentors who know grief well.

- Cultivating gratitude and peace amid all the upheaval and change.

We need to recognize that one of the best gifts we can give to the world is the healthiest us possible. The healthier we are - mentally, emotionally, physically, spiritually, and relationally - the more we can engage in our ultimate mission and purpose.

It's not about being perfect. It's about taking the next step toward taking better care of ourselves. As we travel the grief road and take more steps toward good self-care, our capacity to live well and love others grows and expands.

Our world needs people who know grief and how to navigate loss well. You can be one of those people. So much of life is about overcoming adversity and turning pain into purpose.

If you're struggling with self-care, rest assured that many other grieving hearts are too. For your own sake - and for the sake of those immediately around you - bump good self-care up to the top of your priority list.

Affirmation:

I'll pursue good self-care during this time of loss. I'll pursue personal wellness every day, one step at a time.

Suggestions:

In summary, here are some quick tips to consider for pursuing personal wellness via good self-care:

- Exercise. Get some exercise every day, even if it's walking around your neighborhood. Pursue an exercise regimen that is realistic and fits your current situation and health. Consult a physician or health professional before beginning an exercise program.

- Eat well and hydrate. Take steps toward better nutrition. Make sure you get enough water and electrolytes. Liquid and powdered electrolytes are widely available at grocery stores and online health stores.

- Cultivate gratitude. We're hyperaware of what we've lost and what we're losing. You can balance that with a daily practice of thanksgiving. Begin each day by expressing gratitude for three things you're thankful for. Over time, this practice nurtures your heart and protects it from danger.

Be kind to yourself. Keep self-care in focus. You're more important than you know.

40

HOW DO I KEEP FROM SLIPPING INTO OLD, UNHEALTHY HABITS?

I can feel myself slipping backwards.

The pain is driving me to old, unhealthy habits.

These things promise relief, but they're only quick fixes that never work.

Afterwards, the shame and guilt invade, and I feel worse off than before.

I feel stuck. Trapped.

What can I do?

We all have unhealthy habits back there. Some of us have an entire suitcase full of them.

We all have addictions. These are things we engage in when the stress vice tightens to the point where we feel like we need to escape. Fear is ultimately behind this. Something has happened that has put us in fight-or-flight mode. Some of us have been hit hard enough that we spend a lot of our lives running from or fighting something.

Here are some of the more common addictions in our world today: alcohol, illegal and prescription drugs, tobacco and nicotine, coffee, gambling, pornography, sex, food, the internet and technology, video games, work, spending, collecting, entertainment, exercise, worry and negative thinking, etc.

Almost anything, even good things, can be used to try and medicate our pain and keep our terrors at bay. Our addictive habits become an unhealthy crutch. They are self-sabotaging coping mechanisms that simply do not work.

We might get momentary relief, but the price we pay for it is astronomical. Guilt and shame invade. A sense of failure and worthlessness surface. We get caught in a cycle of slow self-destruction.

Some addictions are more serious than others, of course. But all addictions have their own insidious impact on our hearts, minds, and lives.

As with other challenges on the grief journey, addictions are not something that we can tackle and manage on our own. We need trustworthy people to walk with us through these deep, dark valleys.

No one is immune from addiction. In fact, we all have them, of one form or another.

If you feel yourself slipping back into old, unhealthy habits, please know that this is common in grief. The stress of loss and all the life changes can easily tip us over into the well-worn ruts of addictive behavior. Accepting what is happening is the first step. Then you can respond rather than continuing to react in self-harming cycles.

Avoid isolating at all costs. Be kind to yourself by reaching out for help and assistance.

Release the guilt and shame. Let go of the illusion of control.

Affirmation:

I'll be alert about the power of unhealthy habits. I'll guard my heart by connecting well with people who can walk with me in these dark places.

Suggestions:

Below are some suggestions to consider when unhealthy habits start to exert their influence.

- Reach out for support. Ask yourself, "Who can I contact about this?"

- If you're not already, strongly consider connecting with an organization that specializes in the addictions and unhealthy habits you find yourself struggling with: Celebrate Recovery, Alcoholics Anonymous, Narcotics Anonymous, Gamblers Anonymous, Sex Addicts Anonymous, etc. Check your area for local addiction recovery and support options.

- Consider connecting with a mental health professional who understands addictions and the grief process. An experienced, knowledgeable counselor can be a huge asset during this time.

When stress goes up, unhealthy habits knock louder. Please don't try to tackle this on your own. You need good support to stay on the healthy grief path.

"Look closely and you will see almost everyone carrying bags of cement on their shoulders.

That's why it takes courage to get out of bed in the morning and climb into the day."

—Edward Hirsch

PART FOUR:

THE SPIRITUAL SHAKING

"It's like a thousand needles have
been thrust into my soul.

God seems far, far away.

I don't know what to think, or what to believe."

-Morgan

This section is a tough one.

Things can get heated when we bring God and spiritual things into the grief conversation. Many feel strongly about these issues from a variety of standpoints and faith perspectives.

I personally identify with the Christian faith. I am a follower of Jesus Christ.

I don't pretend to have it all together. I'm terribly fallible and massively limited. My mistakes and failures are numerous. But Jesus is my life, and therefore it's impossible for me to remove Him from my thinking or my writing.

Having said that, I have endeavored to do my best to discuss the issues in this section in a way that will hopefully connect well with you, wherever you might be coming from spiritually.

Whatever your faith or spiritual perspective, my prayer is that you will find many things in the following pages you can relate to and apply to your grief journey.

41

WHAT DO I DO WITH ALL THESE QUESTIONS?

I have questions - lots of them.

Why did this happen?

**What does this all mean? What's
the purpose of all this?**

Is there a purpose? How can I know?

What about God, faith, and the afterlife?

How does this all fit together, or does it?

What do I do with all these questions?

When we lose someone special, sooner or later the questions start to surface. Close losses tend to shake our souls.

We wonder about things. We have questions now that perhaps we didn't have before.

Maybe we thought we knew something, but now we're not so sure. Perhaps we're now surer of certain things, but not of others.

We naturally wonder why this happened. Did it have to happen? Did it have to happen the way it did? Is there a greater purpose behind this loss? If so, what is it?

Where is our friend or loved one now? Is there an after-life? If so, what are they experiencing? Can they see us? Are they watching?

What does this loss mean for us? What do we do now? How do we live? Why are we here? What's our purpose?

Many of us go through life putting these questions aside. Then a loss comes. Our hearts are cracked wide open. Questions start spilling out everywhere.

Our hearts are reeling. We scream that we want answers. Deep down, however, the reality is that very few answers would be emotionally satisfying right now. No answer will reverse time. No answer will bring our friend or loved one back.

And yet, our souls must ask the questions.

As with the other facets of grief, the key is being real with ourselves and hopefully a few other people about what's happening inside us. As we are authentic and honest about our questions, this helps us process our way through them.

Questions with no satisfying answers tend to boomer-ang back - over and over again. Chances are we'll find ourselves wondering about the same things, time and time again. The same questions tend to circle in our minds and hearts like an airplane in a holding pattern waiting for clearance to land.

As we process the loss and express our grief in healthy ways, these circling questions tend to demand less atten-tion. They begin to take their place in our grief journey. We come to the point where we begin to coexist more peacefully with some of them. Other questions might nag us for a very long time.

If you're struggling with some deep soul questions as a result of your loss, please know that this is natural and common. Loss and death shatter our sense of normalcy. Grief shakes our souls.

Affirmation:

This loss has shaken me and raised some deeper questions. I'll give myself permission to ask whatever questions arise and process these wonderings over time.

Suggestions:

Here are some tips for when deep soul questions begin to surface:

- Accept yourself as you are in the moment. This also means accepting yourself with whatever questions might be rolling around in your heart and soul.

- Give yourself permission to ask whatever questions surface. Some questions might be uncomfortable, unnerving, or even frightening. That's okay. If the question is in your mind, it needs to be processed. Your soul questions will express themselves, one way or another.

- Consider making a list of your questions. Be as specific as possible. Just the physical act of recording what you're wondering about will help you process it.

- Share your question list with someone safe you trust. Verbalizing your questions to another person might be uncomfortable and scary, but it can be extremely helpful.

You were designed for relationship and wired for connection. Do your best to connect with loving, compassionate people who can walk with you as you tackle the questions swirling in your soul.

42

WHERE IS GOD IN ALL THIS?

I can't seem to feel God's presence.

God seems so far away, so distant and aloof.

I pray, but I don't think it gets past the ceiling.

Is God there? Does He care?

Where is God in all this?

When loss strikes, many naturally turn to God for help. We're hurting and wounded. Our hearts are broken and crushed. Our lives have been forcefully altered. We look up. We need comfort, perspective, reassurance, and perhaps some answers.

Many feel distant from God during this time. We can't seem to sense His presence. Perhaps our prayers feel stale and empty. At a time when we desperately want to feel God's comfort and hear His voice, all we seem to get is silence.

We wonder where God is in all this. Is He there? Does He care?

We're stunned. Our hearts, minds, and souls are on overload. When stunned and overloaded, it's difficult to perceive things accurately.

Loss and grief are incredibly stressful. We're experiencing soul stress too.

In times of soul stress - and soul distress - God often feels far away simply because our feelers are already maxed out. Just as we experience emotional, mental, and physical fatigue, we can find ourselves spiritually exhausted as well.

One thing is certain: Life is not what it was. Our world has changed. This affects our souls too.

The truth is that we never stay the same spiritually. We live, walk, stumble, heal, and grow. Sometimes we take steps forward spiritually. Other times, we retreat and withdraw. Our spiritual life tends to go back and forth and up and down according to what's happening in our lives.

Since we're human, we tend to make things about us. We make ourselves and how we're doing the center of our personal universe. In times of grief stress, our limited abilities are squeezed. We're hurting. Our pain tends to set the agenda for our thoughts and emotions.

Just because we don't feel His presence doesn't mean God is not with us. Just because we feel distant from God doesn't mean God is distant from us. Just because we're not hearing God's voice at present doesn't mean that He is not speaking. Just because we don't feel God's comfort and love doesn't mean He isn't comforting and loving us right now.

Yes, we would love to feel all this. We would like to feel anything other than this terrible pain and emotional agony. Our feelers are fully occupied with this loss. There's not much of us left, if any, to feel or experience much of anything good. We can only process so much.

Feeling distant from God is common for grieving souls. You can feel like you're in a spiritual wilderness of sorts - a dry and barren place with little to no water.

You're a traveler on the grief journey. You're passing through this awful wilderness, but it is not your destination. This present desert is not your new home.

On we journey, one day, one hour, one moment, one step at a time.

Affirmation:

If I feel empty or distant from God, I'll remember this is common in grief. I'll accept myself and things as they are and journey through this difficult place one step at a time.

Suggestions:

Here are some tips for managing times of soul stress / distress:

- Acknowledge and accept where you are, as you are, even if you feel you're in a spiritually dry and empty wilderness.

- Consider meditation. Take some time and just "be." See yourself in a safe place. Picture yourself releasing angst, anger, and fear. Keep releasing.

- Feelings are important, but they are not necessarily reality. For example, it's possible for a person to feel unloved, yet be deeply loved by many people. It's important to consider the possibility that some of your feelings and perceptions about God at present (His distance, His silence, etc.) may not be accurate. Your feelings are meant to be felt, but they are not always a trustworthy guide for life.

- If you're a praying person, share with God what's going on inside you. Consider praying out loud. This slows your mind down and brings more clarity to your thoughts and emotions. Hearing your own voice can also be helpful. We tend to be able to "release" more if we say things out loud.

- Consider writing your prayers. This gives those circling, cycling thoughts a place to land. Seeing your thoughts on paper (or on a computer screen) can also help settle the mind and heart. "Getting the grief out" can be an important part of prayer and our spiritual life.

- Are there people whose faith and spiritual life you respect and admire? When we consult people like this, we tend to collect invaluable wisdom along the way.

Take the spiritual impact of this loss seriously. Rather than fleeing or fighting what's happening inside you, use it to grieve well, heal, and grow.

43

HOW DO I HANDLE BEING ANGRY WITH GOD?

I'm angry.

Did this have to happen, now, this way? Why?

**My loved one has been taken from me,
and there's nothing I can do.**

Did God do this? Did God allow this?

Surely, He could have stopped this.

**I'm angry with God, and I don't
know what to do with that.**

Anger is extremely prevalent in the grief journey. We're relational creatures designed to love and be loved. When death invades and separation occurs, our hearts and souls scream. Something about this just doesn't make sense to us.

Anger always seeks a target. As our hearts search for answers, it's not unusual for our minds to work their way up the ladder of responsibility and end up targeting God. After all, we reason, the buck ultimately stops with Him.

Our souls wrestle with the possibilities. He could have stopped this. He could have healed them. He could have intervened in some way.

For some of us, even the thought of being angry with God is terrifying. "It's wrong to be mad at God!" we reason. So, we deny our anger and refuse to address our spiritual angst.

For others of us, we have no problem blaming God. He's an easy and convenient target. Wounded and fuming, we walk away from God and want nothing to do with Him.

For still others of us, this loss is proof that God either does not care or does not exist. Life is so full of pain and suffering that it's hard for us to conceive that there is a Supreme Being who is good at the helm of the universe. We can be furious with God, even while we deny His existence.

Accepting what's happening inside in the moment is key in processing spiritual anger. Denying or hiding what's there only gives our anger and angst more power. Eventually, stuffed anger morphs into bitterness and even hatred. Such things only add pain to our already shattered hearts.

If we're angry with God, the healthiest thing to do is to express our angst directly to Him. If He is indeed God, then He knows our hearts already. He is fully aware of our anger.

If we have a personal relationship with God, then owning up to our spiritual anger is vitally important in relating well to Him. Quality relationships are built on openness and trust. If He is a God of relationship and loves us, then He wants us to share openly with Him.

No matter what our spiritual beliefs, hiding or stuffing our anger is ultimately a form of self-punishment. Our raging internal angst will be expressed, one way or another. If we don't let it out in healthy ways, it will end up leaking out in ways that we'll most likely regret.

Anger with God is common for those enduring a close loss. Finding honest and healthy ways to "get it out" becomes vitally important in nurturing and protecting your heart on this painful grief journey.

Affirmation:

If I find myself angry at God, I'll be honest about that and express my angst in healthy ways. I'll continue to be real about what's happening inside me.

Suggestions:

If you find yourself angry with God in your grief process, here are a few options you may want to consider:

- Express your anger with God directly to God in prayer. T.W.A. can be helpful here. Talk it out. Write in out in a journal or perhaps as a prayer. Art it out in a creative way. Be honest with yourself and God by "getting it out." For more information on T.W.A., see the end of chapter 10.

- Share about your anger with a safe person. Let them know what you're going to be venting about and ask them to just listen. There is something about sharing openly with another person that can be especially freeing and healing.

- Perhaps you don't believe in God yet find yourself angry with Him. This is not unusual. Even though you don't believe He exists, try expressing your angst directly to Him. Focus on "getting it out" in healthy ways.

Processing frustration with God is usually not a once-and-done event. As much as possible, try to process things as they surface in your mind, heart, and soul.

44

WHY? WHY? WHY?

Why did this happen?

Did it have to happen? Why?

Why them? Why now? Why this way?

Why me? Why us? Why?

I don't understand.

"Why?" is the number one question that plagues most grieving hearts.

When loss strikes, we're stunned. When we begin to come to our senses, our minds try to make sense of what's happened.

We'll always deny what we're not prepared to accept. At first, we're not anywhere near ready to accept this loss. We don't want to. We don't want this to be real.

Our hearts and souls keep circling back to "Why?"

Part of the trouble is that "Why?" in itself is an intellectual question. Even though our minds are trying to make sense of the loss intellectually, it's ultimately our hearts and souls asking the question. "Why?" becomes deeply emotional in nature.

In other words, even if we could intellectually under-stand "Why?", most likely the answer would not satisfy our broken hearts.

No answer will bring back our friend or loved one. No answer can take away the pain of loss. No answer can turn back time and give us a do-over.

Though there may not be an emotionally satisfying answer, our souls must ask this powerful three-letter question repeatedly. Question-asking is a crucial and nec-essary part of the grief journey.

The more close, traumatic losses we've endured in life, the more the question "Why?" tends to surface and shake us. In the case of multiple losses, processing and grieving each loss individually is important. See chapter 29 for a detailed discussion of how to handle multiple losses.

"Why?" can lead to new spiritual questioning. We're as-saulted by doubts and wonderings. If left unexpressed or unprocessed, "Why?" can catapult us into a faith crisis. More on that in the next chapter.

If you find yourself repeatedly asking "Why?", rest as-sured that this is natural and common for those grieving a close loss. Be honest with yourself and accept yourself where you are. Work on "getting the grief out" by express-ing "Why?" in healthy ways.

Affirmation:

"Why?" is a common question in grief. I'll be honest with myself, God, and safe people about my questions and process them as best I can.

Suggestions:

Here are some suggestions to consider when the question "Why?" comes knocking:

- Practice breathing deeply. "Why?" can be an anxiety-producing, anxiety-driven question. Deep breathing can be extremely helpful in managing the more anxious moments in grief. For more info on deep breathing as a grief skill, see the end of chapter five.

- Use T.W.A. to express and process your "Why?" questions. Talk it out. Write down your "Why?" questions. Be as specific as possible. "Get it out." Creatively use art to express your "Why?" A detailed explanation of T.W.A. can be found in the last part of chapter 10.

- If you have a relationship with God, be honest with Him about your "Why?" questions. Try praying out loud. Let yourself hear your own voice sharing your heart and your frustrations. A healthy relationship with God operates on honesty and trust.

- Be real with a safe person about your "Why?" questions. You might feel shy or embarrassed about this. Taking the risk to be real and share is far preferable to stuffing these important issues deep inside.

Though you might not get satisfying answers, your heart needs to express its questions. Be honest. Stay open. Be patient with yourself.

45

WHAT DO I DO WITH ALL MY DOUBTS?

I used to know what I believed.

**Now, I'm not so sure. Every-
thing seems so uncertain.**

My soul is suddenly packed with doubt.

My faith is in crisis.

How do I navigate this?

Heavy loss can shake our souls to the point where we have a faith crisis. What we thought we believed is being challenged by the intense shock, pain, and upheaval of loss.

Along the road of life, most of our beliefs will be challenged at some juncture. The pressures, stresses, and losses we encounter batter and crush simplistic clichés and shallow platitudes. Suffering squeezes our souls and causes us to think more deeply about what we believe.

In times of loss, many of us feel disappointed or let down by God. Some of us can even feel abandoned or rejected by Him. Our beliefs about His plan, His goodness, and His love can be shaken or crushed. It can seem as if the rope that anchored our souls has been cut, and we suddenly find ourselves drifting to who knows where.

If we're not honest with ourselves, God, and perhaps a few others about what's happening inside us, these doubts can multiply exponentially. Our sense of safety, security, and hope can be rattled or even shattered. Our frustration, anger, and loneliness can deepen and grow.

As with other aspects of grief, acknowledging what's happening is the first step. We focus on accepting ourselves as we are, in the moment. We've lost someone special. Our hearts are broken. The pain is immense.

We breathe deeply and remind ourselves that now is not forever. Just because we feel betrayed, forsaken, and alone doesn't mean this is so. Yet we do feel this way, and we need to take those feelings seriously and process them well.

We give ourselves permission to struggle. Questions and doubts do not have to lead to dark places, new terrors, or a rejection of what we once believed. Properly processed, our doubts can lead us to greater healing, growth, and even deeper faith.

We need a faith that is sufficient to deal with the suffering and pain that occurs in the world and in our lives. No shallow, uniformed faith will make the cut. Lasting, resilient faith is almost always forged in the fire of difficulty and hardship.

If you find yourself tussling with doubt and wondering what you really believe, you're in good company. Many grieving hearts wonder and struggle with these things. Loss hits us at the core of our being, and that includes our souls and our faith.

Be patient with yourself. Express this intense grief, complete with all the questions and doubts. "Get it out."

Affirmation:

It is not unusual for loss to lead to a faith crisis. I'll be honest with myself, God, and at least one safe person about what's happening in my heart and soul.

Suggestions:

If you find yourself troubled by spiritual questions and doubts, you might want to consider some of the following:

- Make a list of your questions and doubts. Be as specific as possible. Just the act of "getting it out" in this way can be relieving.

- Read your list out loud. If you feel you have a relationship with God, picture Him there with you. Release the doubts and questions to Him one by one. If you don't feel like you have a relationship with God, just hearing your own voice saying these things can bring perspective.

- Consider sharing your list with someone you trust. Hidden doubts and fears tend to get more powerful and exert great influence. Doubts and fear that are shared can be discussed, processed, and worked through.

- Consider sharing your list with someone you admire and respect spiritually. We need people who can speak into our lives with love and compassion. The perspective of others who have your best interests in mind can be invaluable.

Working through questions, doubts, and fears is not a once-and-done checklist item. This journey will be bumpy. Hang on. Keep your seat belt fastened. Be patient with yourself.

46

CAN LOSS PRODUCE SPIRITUAL FATIGUE?

I don't know what to think, believe, or do.

I feel like someone came along with an eraser and wiped my life clean.

I feel blank, empty, and lost.

I'm overwhelmed by it all and I don't feel like I have anything left inside.

I'm exhausted. Even my soul is tired.

When loss hits our souls, the results can be deep and lasting. One of the most immediate results is a sense of spiritual fatigue.

The heaviness and intensity of the grief journey can be incredibly draining. We can quickly become emotionally, physically, mentally, and spiritually fatigued. Spiritual exhaustion is real, and it is common in the grief process.

There comes a point where the fatigue is so heavy, we begin to shut down. We need a break. We don't have the energy to deal with the overwhelming cloud of fear of uncertainty that surrounds us. We barely have the strength to eat, much less to pray, think, or engage in anything else heavy.

Perhaps we engage in some spiritual activities or faith family gatherings. After a loss, this can feel awkward and complicated. Our lives have changed, but everyone else's life appears to be moving along as usual. This new disconnect can be disturbing and drain our energies even further. The sheer amount of change we're enduring is exhausting.

Simply put, we're worn out.

How do we deal with this?

We could try increasing our activity, but that takes more energy. We could try to figure it out, but our mental capacity is already being squeezed. We could "try harder spiritually" (whatever that means), but our tanks are already empty.

When exhausted, the usual prescription that leads to healing involves rest and receiving.

We need down time. We need rest. We need space and margin in our lives more than ever.

When our tank is empty, we need to begin to fill it. We need to find ways to receive good things during this time. Grieving hearts need good, encouraging, hope-giving inflow.

If you're experiencing spiritual fatigue, rest assured that this is natural and common on this taxing grief journey. Your heart and soul are feeling the weight of the loss.

Be kind to yourself. Get the down time you need. Manage your inflow so that your tank gets filled a bit rather than even further drained. Learn to both rest and receive.

Affirmation:

When spiritual fatigue hits, I'll be kind to myself by learning to both rest and receive. I'll get the down time I need and seek good inflow during this draining season of grief.

Suggestions:

When you experience spiritual fatigue, here are a few tips that might be helpful:

- Accept yourself where you are. It's okay to be spiritually drained. Give yourself permission to not see things perfectly or even accurately when exhausted. Embrace the spiritual fatigue as part of your heart expressing your love for the one you lost.

- Look at your schedule and consider your current expectations of yourself. Where can you create some space and margin for rest and receiving? What can you let go of or offload to someone else? What is necessary, and what can wait?

- What kinds of things and people seem to bring rest and refreshment to your soul? Make a list. Create some space in your life for these people and activities. These rest-and-refreshment-givers can greatly enhance your soul health.

- Consider your current "inflow." What influences are you subjected to daily? These influences usually come in two main forms: people and information. We need good, healthy people and influences in our lives right now. How can you manage your "inflow" to maximize the good and minimize the unhelpful?

Spiritual fatigue is real. Many grieving hearts experience it. Breathe. Rest. Receive.

47

IS SPIRITUAL NUMBNESS A PART OF GRIEF?

I feel numb.

I feel numb emotionally and spiritually.

This should be frightening, but it's like I can't feel the fear - or I don't care.

I hope this gets better, because I don't want to be like this.

Is spiritual numbness a thing? Is it a part of grief?

Yes, it's possible to be spiritually numb.

When our feelers shut down, it can be disconcerting and even frightening. If we normally feel close to God or spiritually connected, this change can be alarming indeed. Our souls scream, "No! I can't afford to lose this too!"

And yet, when we're numb, a part of us just doesn't seem to care anymore. We're "zoned out" spiritually. We're going through the motions. Our heart feels disconnected, or perhaps altogether absent.

Fellow grievers describe feeling like an "emotional zombie" or "an empty soul." The pain of the loss has pummeled our entire being to the point that we aren't able to enjoy or even engage in areas that are typically life-giving to us.

The truth is that our souls and hearts have not departed. They are still intact and functioning. We're still feeling and sensing many things, but life is such that we can't fully experience them in the moment. Our spiritual life hasn't disappeared, but our awareness and appreciation of it has been dulled by the pain of loss.

Loss comes with a phenomenal amount of change. These changes were not our choice. Our lives were altered without our consent or permission. It can feel like we've been acted upon or stolen from. The grinding pressure of constant grief can deaden our spiritual sensors over time.

We go numb.

If you experience a sense of spiritual numbness, please know that this is common for many grieving hearts. Try not to catastrophize your current reality, but instead accept it for what it is - a temporary state. As you get the space and time you need to rest, most likely your spiritual desire will return.

Be patient with yourself. Tell yourself, "This is a time of change. This spiritual numbness will change too."

Affirmation:

If I find myself spiritually numb, I'll remember that this is temporary. My heart and soul are tired from managing all this change.

Suggestions:

Spiritual numbness can be alarming for some. If you find yourself "numbed out" spiritually, here are some things to consider:

- It's okay to feel spiritually numb at present. As you give yourself permission to be where you are, over time this numbness will most likely recede.

- Do what you can to get good rest. Too much activity, stress, and sleep deprivation can be a truly formidable and even temporarily debilitating combination. You need space, margin, and rest.

- Beware of isolation. You need to be connected to healthy, trustworthy people, now more than ever. Even though you might feel numb, try reaching out and expressing what you're experiencing along with any concerns you might have.

- Write about the spiritual numbness you're experiencing. List any concerns or worries you might have. Be as specific as you can. Afterwards, try reading your list out loud. Then close your eyes and picture yourself releasing some of the numbness and heaviness.

Feeling spiritually numb can be concerning and even frightening. Be kind to yourself and do what you can to process this well.

48

HOW CAN I FIND HOPE?

I'm sad and distraught.

I'm angry and frustrated.

My world has become dark.

It's almost as if hope has departed somehow.

How can I find hope again?

When a close, painful loss strikes, a domino effect of change begins. The initial loss spawns many others. Like ocean waves, the unwanted changes just keep rolling in.

We have no control over these waves. Each wave is different. Some are stronger than others. Some we can see coming, while others surprise us.

After a while, fatigue sets in and exhaustion is not far behind. All of life becomes about somehow surviving in this new ocean we find ourselves in.

The world around us looks the same, but inside we know that everything is different. Happiness and joy have fled and appear to be things of the past. Life is now heavy. Our world feels empty and dark. Hope can seem to have disappeared.

When our sense of hope fades, other things immediately invade and attempt to fill the vacancy. Depression and despair come knocking.

We acknowledge what's happening inside us. "Hope seems to have been taken from me." "Hope appears to have left." "It feels like hope has abandoned me."

The key words in the above statements are "seems," "appears," and "feels like." Just like "I feel alone" and "I am alone" are two different things, so "My sense of hope seems to be gone" and "Hope is no more" are vastly different.

The truth is that hope is always here. There are times, however, when we don't have eyes to see it. Our minds, hearts, and even souls - all our internal real estate - are being gobbled up by loss and grief. Our vision is blurred at present.

Even if we think there is no hope for us, we will readily admit that there's hope for other people. So somewhere deep down, we know that hope is there. It just doesn't seem to be available for us at the moment.

At some point, it's wise to ask ourselves, "What is my hope in anyway?" We all tend to place hope in someone or something. A spouse, a parent, a child, a friend, etc. A job, money, our health, our abilities, etc. We naturally place at least some of our hope in our situations, circumstances, and relationships. The downside is that when any of these things are threatened or taken from us, our sense of hope takes a nosedive.

Over 3000 years ago, wise King Solomon said, "Hope deferred makes the heart sick, but a longing fulfilled is a tree of life." When hope is delayed somehow, our hearts tend to plummet. When our sense of hope is strong, we thrive inside.

If your sense of hope has taken a hit, take heart that this is a common experience for those on the grief journey. Even though you can't perceive it like you once did, hope is still there. As you process your grief in healthy ways, it's likely your sense of hope will return.

Affirmation:

I'll remember the truth that hope is always there, though my pain and grief may blind me to its presence. I'll do what I can to process this loss in healthy ways and trust my sense of hope will return over time.

Suggestions:

A temporary perception that hope has fled is common following a heavy, close loss. Here are a few tips that might help you navigate this:

- Consider writing down some of what you hoped for that you now consider to be impossible or highly unlikely. Be as specific as possible. Identifying your "lost hopes" more specifically can help you grieve these great disappointments.

- Think about the world and people around you. What do people you know tend to put their hope in? What do you think they hope for? Write these down. Are these "hopes" permanent or temporary? Do the things we tend to put our hope in last forever, or are they only for a time? Most of what we hope for (or put our hope in) is fragile and temporary.

- Wise King Solomon also said, "God has placed eternity in the human heart; yet we do not understand the beginning from the end." We long for a forever good - for a life that isn't marred by trouble, pain, and loss. Do you sense this longing for something more, something eternal, deep within you? If so, what will you do with that longing?

Don't be afraid to look deep inside. We all have things hidden within that we are reluctant to address. Your heart is your most valuable possession. Take good care of your heart.

49

WHY AM I HERE?

This loss has shattered my world and my illusions.

**I was moving, but I'm not sure
I was going anywhere.**

My questions are larger and deeper now.

Why are we here? What is this all about?

Why am I here? What's my purpose?

Sir William Wallace reportedly once said, "Every man dies. Not every man truly lives." We can all relate to this.

We've all had the experience of going through the motions and almost mindlessly moving from one task to another. We get stuck in cycles of doing what we think we're supposed to do to get what we think we want. We march through life carrying an unseen burden of expectations - both our own and what we believe others' expectations to be. The demands placed on us by ourselves and others can blind us to what's really important.

At several junctures in life, most of us have those "Aha!" moments when we realize we're moving but not really living. We've been stuck on a treadmill. We've been working hard and making good time, but we suddenly realize we're not going anywhere.

Loss upends our world. The death of a loved one or friend shatters our routine and knocks us off our treadmill. We find ourselves face down on the ground - stunned, bruised, and wounded. We wonder what happened, how, and why.

As we stumble and stagger forward, we begin to wonder about a lot of things. What is this all about, anyway? Why are we here? What's our purpose?

Loss tends to raise our eyes above the mundane details of life. Most of us find ourselves staring at larger questions that we're usually too busy to contemplate.

Our minds are seeking to understand life better. Our hearts are searching for important answers. Our souls are yearning for something beyond the long to-do lists and rubrics we've been using to maintain a sense of control in life.

When we lack a clear sense of identity and purpose, we live confused lives. Without an understanding of who we are and why we're here, we wander and falter.

And yet, even with all the loss and pain, the crucial importance of people, relationships, love, and service remains. Whatever else we might happen to think or believe, our identity, purpose, and mission includes these four components.

Seasons of loss can be times of self-evaluation. On the grief journey, many allow their pain and grief to lead them to live with greater passion and purpose. Inevitably, people, relationships, love, and service end up being a huge part of that.

If you're wondering more about who you are and why you're here, you're in good company. Many grieving hearts tussle with this.

Affirmation:

I'll stay open to what this loss might teach about who I am and why I'm here. Though I might not know how, I'll trust that it's possible that I can live with more purpose and meaning than ever before.

Suggestions:

Knowing your purpose, why you are here, forms the basis for all you do. Below are some tips to consider as you tussle with this during a time of loss:

- Consider contemplating and writing down why you're here. Try to define, as clearly as possible, your purpose. Whatever our personal missions are, we know that they will include people, relationships, love, and service.

- As you think about your purpose and mission, this may naturally bring up all you've lost along the way. Chances are there are many things about the loss of your friend or loved one which are tied to your sense of why you are here. Consider using T.W.A. (talk it out, write it out, art it out) to express your grief about what you've lost.

- Once you define your purpose a bit more clearly, this can help you with daily decision-making. Let your purpose - why you are here - guide your routine and activities.

Loss can shake your sense of meaning and purpose. Embrace this as an opportunity to contemplate why you are here and align your life accordingly.

"Well, everyone can master a grief but he that has it."

—William Shakespeare

PART FIVE:

THE RELATIONAL SHIFTS

"People are treating me differently.
My relationships are changing. I can feel it.
I feel lost and alone."
-Stephanie

50

WHERE DID EVERYONE GO?

People I counted on disappeared.

Everyone was supportive at first.

Then, poof. No calls. No emails. No texts.

What happened?

I feel abandoned.

Where did everyone go?

People don't know what to do with grief. This is strange considering we all deal with loss along the way. We assume that those around us will be compassionate, concerned, and supportive. Sadly, this is often not the case.

Many grieving hearts feel at least somewhat abandoned by the people they had counted on for support. Some people tend to disappear or almost evaporate into thin air. One minute they're expressing concern, and the next minute they are inexplicably absent.

We don't get the calls we hoped for. We don't get the emails and texts we had expected. Once the funeral is over, everyone goes back to their own lives while we're left on the outside looking in. We were once a part of all this. Now, we exist in an alternate universe clouded with emotional pain and grief.

We've talked about the fact that we're clearly designed for relationship and wired for connection. This is partially why the death of a close friend or loved one is so painful. When others seem to distance themselves when we need them the most, our hearts are once again shocked and stunned.

Most people have trouble being in the presence of loss and grief. No one enjoys suffering or watching someone they care about endure personal pain. We unconsciously avoid situations that we sense will be emotionally challenging or uncomfortable.

In some senses these "disappearances" aren't particularly surprising, yet the lack of contact and expressions of support from those who say they care about us is also profoundly confusing and disappointing. This adds to our sadness and can stoke our anger. No wonder many grieving hearts feel alone.

If people you counted on seem to be distancing themselves from you, please remember that this is far more about them than about you and your loss. What you're experiencing from them is disappointing and painful, but it is also extremely common for those traveling the grief road.

Keep breathing deeply. Be kind to yourself. Care and support are out there, but it may not come from those you anticipated.

Affirmation:

If people I counted on disappear, I'll remember that their lack of response is more about them than about me. The support I need is out there, but it might not come from whom I expect.

Suggestions:

If people you counted on for support aren't showing up, rest assured that many grieving hearts experience this. Here are a few suggestions that might help you navigate this challenge:

- Accept where you are, as you are, in the present moment. Acknowledge that you don't control how people respond to you and your grief. Remind yourself that their responses are more about them than about you.

- Do what you can to express the emotions and thoughts that are running around inside you. Talk it out. Write it out. Art it out. Consider sharing your frustrations with a safe person who is a great listener. For more info on T.W.A., please see the end of chapter 10.

- Consider writing a letter to these people (one that you will never send). Let it rip. Be honest and uncensored. "Get it out" so that this frustration doesn't build up and fester into something even more challenging.

- For the sake of your own heart, consider forgiving those who have disappointed you. We'll talk more about forgiveness, including what it is and what it isn't, in subsequent chapters.

Relationships are messy and often painful. Breathe deeply and expect relational upset during this season of loss.

51

WHY ARE PEOPLE TREATING ME THIS WAY?

I don't get it.

**I naturally expect people, especially those
who know me, to be kind and respectful.**

Instead, they judge me.

**They say and do unhelpful things
- even mean things.**

What did I do to deserve this?

Why are people treating me this way?

The world is not kind to grieving hearts.

Frankly, grief scares people. We flee from suffering like it's the plague. If anything emotionally uncomfortable comes our way, we quickly bar the door. We attempt to ignore it and pretend it's not there. When we can't do that, we fight against it by saying and doing unhelpful and even hurtful things.

Loss is a universal experience. Every human being endures staggering losses, some from an early age. We get hit again and again in life. Over time, the losses build up.

Instead of dealing with these losses and embracing the grief involved, many choose to ignore them and push on. More loss comes and adds even more weight to their already heavy baggage. Just as they deny the pain of loss in their own life, they also do the same when confronted by the losses of others.

When someone is uncomfortable in the presence of our grief, chances are our pain is triggering theirs. Most don't know what to do with this, and so they spout platitudes and spew advice. Not willing to look at their own grief, they quickly jump to fixing ours.

Judgment from those around us only adds to our sense of loss.

Knowing whom we can and can't trust in the grief process is important. Most of us learn over time who is going to be supportive and who isn't. We need to be careful about being vulnerable and sharing what's inside us with those who will not respect our grief. We need to guard our already broken hearts.

This brings up a key principle of healthy grieving: Connect well with those who are helpful to you and limit your exposure to those who aren't.

When you feel misunderstood, judged, and even rejected, please know that this is a common experience for those walking the grief path. Some people won't understand. Some won't even try.

Rather than receiving this sense of rejection and letting it poison your heart, learn to forgive. Being able to release offenses quickly protects your heart. Forgiving is a way of saying, "I will not let these hurtful looks, attitudes, and comments control or overly influence my life."

We'll talk more about forgiveness in the next chapter.

Affirmation:

When I feel misunderstood, belittled, or rejected by others, chances are my grief is triggering theirs. I'll be kind to myself and protect my heart by forgiving quickly.

Suggestions:

Almost every grieving heart experiences some frustration, friction, and rejection in their relationships. When this happens in your life, here are some tips to consider:

- How can you help yourself remember that how people respond to you is more about them than it is about you?

- Process any painful interactions you have with others on your grief journey. Write it out in a journal or in letters that you will never send. Try writing some poetry. The more you express this relational pain and "get it out" in healthy ways, the less hold it will have on you.

- How can you get around people who are helpful to you and limit your exposure to those who aren't? What would this look like for you? What do you sense is the next step? Who is helpful to you, and who is not?

- Picture the person who has offended you. What would it mean for you to forgive and release them so that what they said or did doesn't further damage your heart?

People will make all the difference in your grief process - one way or the other. Limiting the influence of unsupportive people will help guard your heart from additional pain and frustration.

52

HOW DO I FORGIVE THOSE WHO HAVE HURT ME?

**Loss is painful enough with-
out other people adding to it.**

**Unkind comments and actions swirl in
my mind and plague me at night.**

My anger level is rising.

**I want to lash out and give them a dose
of their own medicine somehow.**

People tell me I need to let it go and to forgive.

How do I forgive those who have hurt me?

What is forgiveness anyway?

Our natural tendency is often to treat others the way they have treated us.

Of course, this usually makes matters worse. We're angered by what they've said or done, and then try to get back at them by playing their game. We try to fight fire with fire instead of using a fire extinguisher.

The fire extinguisher in this case is forgiveness.

Forgiveness is not for the other person (the offending party). We can't do anything about their fire. We can only deal with our fire. Sparks have drifted over from their inferno and have ignited something in us.

Forgiveness is not saying that it didn't hurt or that it didn't matter. Forgiveness is saying that it did hurt and that it does matter. In fact, it matters enough that we will not let their sparks fuel our fire.

Forgiveness is releasing the other person so that what they said and did doesn't control or overly influence us. Forgiveness is saying, "I release what you did and said because I don't want that in my life."

Forgiveness is proactively guarding yourself against further pain and future bitterness by returning the offense to its owner. Forgiveness says, "What you did and said is more about you than about me. I return to you what is yours because it's not healthy for me."

When we refuse to be drawn into the back-and-forth trap and treat others the way we ourselves **want** to be treated, we take leaps forward that we're unaware of. When we forgive, we leave their words hanging in the air. Perhaps they will realize what they've done. Perhaps not. We're not in control of that.

Forgiveness is choosing to live above what is said or done to you. You become the standard-setter rather than the reactor.

Forgiveness is simple, but hard. We must release our own pride and do what is good rather than reacting by doing what is natural.

Forgiveness is a choice that takes care of you and honors your loved one. This choice guards your heart.

Forgiveness is a crucial healing skill for those on the grief journey.

Affirmation:

When I'm offended by something others said or did, I'll breathe deeply and try to forgive quickly. I will release unhelpful words and actions that might damage my heart.

Suggestions:

Here is a forgiveness exercise you might want to consider:

- Begin by breathing deeply. Breathe slowly in through your nose and out through your mouth for at least a minute. For a detailed explanation of this important grief skill, see the end of chapter five.

- Picture yourself in a safe place. Perhaps this is a place from your past where you felt loved and protected. Keep breathing deeply.

- Once you feel calm, picture the person who offended you. See them in your mind's eye.

- Talk to them. Say what you want to say. Share with them how you feel. Keep breathing deeply.

- When you sense you've said what you want and need to, tell them, "I will not allow what you said or did to rule my heart. I forgive and release you. I return to you what is yours." See yourself releasing their words and actions.

- Finish by spending another minute or so breathing deeply.

This exercise has been extremely helpful to many. Give it a try. In the future, when you feel anger rising within you about something someone did or said, go through this process. Don't let what others say and do rule your life or your grief process.

Forgiveness is simple but hard. Do the hard but healthy and healing thing. Forgive. Release. And then keep forgiving.

53

HOW DO I RESPOND TO OTHERS' HURTFUL COMMENTS?

I can't believe what some people will say.

I don't expect people to understand, but I would like some common human decency here.

Why can't people be quiet?

Why do they have to say anything at all?

What do I do with this?

How do I respond to the hurtful comments of those around me?

When people are uncomfortable, they tend to say unhelpful and even hurtful things. At a time when we need compassion, comfort, and reassurance, these unfeeling comments can stun and slice us.

Our tendency is to respond in kind and confront these callous statements. Insensitive comments often come from wounded, frustrated, and angry hearts. When confronted, such people tend to fire back in anger. It's almost as if they are looking for a fight.

Others, believe it or not, have no idea they're being insensitive. They think they're helping. Perhaps they're simply parroting what they've heard others say in similar situations. "At least they're not suffering anymore." "At least they're in a better place now." "At least you had them as long as you did." "At least you're still young and can find someone else." "At least..."

Life is heavy enough already. We certainly don't want to add more baggage by how we react to the insensitivity of others. If possible, we want to respond in ways that are helpful to us - and to the other person - rather than simply react.

Many find it helpful to come up with a few canned responses for times like this. Being proactive and thinking through this beforehand can be massively relieving and empowering.

We might say something like, "I'm struggling right now, and that's okay," or "It's very hard right now, but that's to be expected." "Thank you for your concern," and "I'm missing my loved one, and it hurts," are two more examples.

Depending on what's been said, a powerful response can be to say nothing at all. We might simply look at the speaker and smile. This leaves the callous comment hanging in the air. This might help them consider more deeply what they've said.

Whatever we say needs to be true, short, and succinct. We don't need an argument or even an extended interaction with someone who isn't willing to engage with us in a respectful manner.

It's healthy to put up a boundary with a true, canned response. Perhaps they will recognize how their words came across and be willing to learn. Then we can make the choice about how much we want to engage with them.

Have people said unkind, insensitive things to you? Having some canned responses ready when someone says something insensitive can be a huge benefit in the future.

Affirmation:

I'll choose a few short, canned responses for when others say something unhelpful or insensitive. Rather than being fearful, I can be proactive and prepared for difficult interactions.

Suggestions:

Relationships are normally challenging. When we're grieving, the degree of difficulty tends to go way up. Having a few canned responses ready can be extremely helpful.

- Identify some insensitive comments that have been said to you so far. Write these down.

- Look at the first comment you wrote down. Close your eyes and see the person who said this in front of you. Ask yourself, "What kind of canned response would be good here?"

- The canned response needs to be true, short, and succinct. You want to set a boundary, not start a fight. Don't try to educate them. Focus on guarding your heart. Write down a possible response to this person. Then repeat this process with the rest of the hurtful comments you identified.

As you respond to unhelpful comments with calm, true, short, canned responses, you'll be protecting your heart and also holding others accountable for their words.

54

WHY DOESN'T ANYONE TALK ABOUT THEM?

I'm frustrated and angry.

No one mentions my loved one.

No one even speaks their name.

It's like they never even existed.

Why doesn't anyone talk about them?

After someone special dies, they become the proverbial elephant in every room we enter.

We're always thinking about them. We carry them in our hearts wherever we go. We're hyperaware of their absence. When those we know well see or contact us, they too feel the presence of this unseen elephant.

Yet, no one brings them up. No one even mentions their name. They smile, ask us how we're doing, and make small talk. The whole thing feels awkward and contrived. Normal, everyday interactions become weird and stilted.

It's like we're suddenly made of glass and extremely fragile. Everyone keeps their distance emotionally and tiptoes around us. Most of the time, this is simply because they don't know what to do or say, and they don't want to cause us more pain. The reality is, however, that we end up feeling even more sad, lonely, and unsupported.

Through all of this, our hearts are bursting at the seams. We desperately want to hear our loved one or friend's name. We want to talk about them. We want others to share and talk about them too. The silence feels cold, disrespectful, and terribly insensitive.

Doesn't anyone care? Doesn't anyone else miss them? Why isn't anyone acknowledging what happened?

These other people might be grieving inside, but we would never know. The pervasive silence only adds to our sense of emptiness.

What do we do with this?

We could simply and truthfully ask, "Do you ever think about them? Would you mind if we talked about them some?"

We might say, "I'm missing them badly. Would you mind if I just shared a little?"

Perhaps we choose to simply speak their name ourselves and see what kind of response we get.

This is hard. We're already feeling fragile and vulnerable. Though every interaction might feel risky, we need to remember that there are people out there who would listen and share memories if they only knew that we needed that. Asking for what we want can be scary, but we're also giving those around us a chance to grieve too. It can be a win for everyone.

Find ways to speak their name. Share memories with those who will listen and invite them to do the same.

Affirmation:

I'll speak their name and share their story often and with whomever will listen. By asking others to share their memories, I give us a chance to grieve together.

Suggestions:

If others never mention your loss, here are a few tips to help:

- Try to accept others where they are, as they are. Accepting reality will empower you to decide how you want to respond. Perhaps they're struggling inside too.

- How might you bring up the subject of the "elephant in the room"? Think through some scenarios in your mind. How might you bring your loved one or friend into the conversation?

- Think about your routine. How might you speak their name and share their story amid your everyday life?

- If you haven't already, consider a grief support group. Loved one's names are spoken, and their stories are shared often in these groups. Fellow grievers get it in ways other people don't. Check with local hospices, churches, and healthcare organizations. There are many online options available as well.

Speaking your loved one or friend's name and sharing your memories of them is crucial to a healthy grief process.

55

HOW DO I FIND PEOPLE WHO ARE SUPPORTIVE AND HELPFUL?

Everyone I know is treating me different.

I don't feel accepted or supported.

**My relationships were not what
I thought they were.**

I'm sad, frustrated, angry, and lonely.

**Are there any helpful, supportive people
out there? How do I find them?**

We need loving, supportive people in our lives, especially when we're hurting. Grieving hearts quickly discover, however, that not everyone is kind and understanding. Even close friends and family we counted on can distance themselves or turn judgmental.

Life is about relationships, and people will have a massive impact on our grief journey, in one way or another. We need support from others, perhaps even more than we realize.

How do we find the helpful, supportive people we need?

It's important to remember that there are indeed compassionate people out there who can and will walk with us through this. If we've experienced enough relational disappointment, we can begin to doubt this and find ourselves thinking, "I'm on my own."

Though grief is naturally lonely, we were never meant to walk through this deep valley alone. We need safe people. We need people who can enter our world and be with us in our grief.

Safe people don't belittle us. They don't toss clichés and platitudes at our gaping wounds. They don't try to fix the unfixable. They don't give us advice we haven't asked for.

Safe people are good listeners. They can be quiet in the presence of suffering. They accept us where we are, as we are, in the moment. When we're with them, our hearts begin to relax.

We need to remember, however, that no one is perfect. Even safe people have lapses and make mistakes. Safe people are also affected by the stress in their lives and the pressures from the world around them. Just as they give us grace, we need to be ready to extend grace to them as well.

Often the best way to find safe people is to focus on being a safe person. As we become people who accept others as they are in the moment, we tend to recognize others who do the same. The better listeners we become, the better we recognize other good listeners.

Safe people tend to find each other. They are drawn to one another like a magnet.

There are safe, supportive people out there. Begin to look for them, and focus on being a safe, supportive person yourself along the way.

Affirmation:

I'll seek the safe, supportive people I need while focusing on becoming a safe, supportive person myself. Together, we will get through this.

Suggestions:

If you find yourself wondering how to find safe, supportive people in your grief process, here are a few things to consider:

- Think for a moment about the definition of a "safe person" as described in this chapter. Among those you know, who seems safe to you?

- How might you connect regularly with these safe people? Put this high on your priority list. Regular contact with safe people over time can make a huge difference in your grief process.

- Would you consider yourself to be a safe person for others? If not, how might you begin to become more "safe?" Working toward becoming more of a safe person is a wonderful pursuit and will help you heal and grow.

You need safe people in your life. Others need you in their lives. Healthy, safe relationships can go a long way in helping all of us adjust, recover, heal, and grow.

56

HOW DO I WORK WELL WHILE GRIEVING?

To say that work is a challenge is
a gross understatement.

On the one hand, I'm glad to have something to do.

On the other hand, I feel like I'm going through
the motions just trying to get through the day.

Coworkers are watching me and probably judging my performance.

My bosses are sending signals that they
want me back to normal yesterday.

How do I handle this? How do I
work well while grieving?

———————————

Work is normally a challenge. When we're grieving, just getting through the workday can seem like an unassisted, solo swim of the Pacific.

Our boss and coworkers will most likely be sympathetic and compassionate for a while. It won't be long, however, before they are ready for us to "move on," "get over it", and get back to normal.

The trouble is that our old normal is gone. Our lives have been altered. We're different now. We're grieving, adjusting, and changing every day. We won't be who we were before.

This leaves us in a sort of work limbo. We're there and we're trying, but at the same time we're not all there and our performance is certainly not what it was. We're more emotional. We tire more easily. We zone out from time to time. We forget details. We're desperately trying to keep up even though our hearts are in a million pieces.

It would be great if bosses, supervisors, and coworkers recognized the overwhelming power of a close loss and adjusted their expectations of us for a while. In a few rare cases, that might happen. For most of us, however, the expectation is that it's business as usual, even though our lives are completely different.

We sense coworkers are watching us. Perhaps they wonder how we're doing. Maybe they're frustrated that we don't seem to be pulling our weight right now. We wonder if they're collectively judging us and talking about us behind our backs.

If possible, good communication with our boss, supervisor, and coworkers can go a long way toward easing some of this workplace tension. Sitting down with those we work closely with and talking a bit about our loss and what it means for our work can be uncomfortable and scary. Having the vulnerable, honest conversation, however, can do wonders at increasing understanding and improving teamwork.

In sports, successful teams plan for and then adjust to player injuries. When one player is limited for a time, other players step up and fill in the gap. Ideally, working on a team should be the same. Part of working well together is being willing to adjust for the unseen upsets that will inevitably occur.

If you find work extra challenging right now, remind yourself that is to be expected. Be patient with yourself and focus on taking one thing, one step, one moment at a time.

Affirmation:

Work and heavy grief are a challenging combo. I'll do what I can to take care of myself by adjusting my expectations of myself and communicating well with coworkers.

Suggestions:

After a close loss, our work performance will be affected, perhaps in many ways. The goal is not to perform as usual, but rather work as well as possible, given where you are in your grief process. Below are some suggestions that might help:

- Consider having an open, honest conversation with your boss or supervisor about your loss and about work expectations. Perhaps they will ask what they or other coworkers can do to help. Even if they offer nothing, you've had the conversation, and that's very important - both for you and for them.

- Check in with your boss or supervisor on a regular basis - once a week perhaps - just to update them about how things are going. Ongoing communication is key to long-term success.

- Consider giving your boss or work mates a copy of **Please Be Patient I'm Grieving: How to Care for and Support the Grieving Heart**. This easy-to-read book will help them understand you and others who are grieving.

- Adjust your expectations of yourself. Keep your to-do list short and manageable.

Pursue open, honest communication at work when you can with whom you can. Be patient with yourself and others. Now is not business as usual for you.

57

WHAT DO I DO IF GRIEF IS AFFECTING MY MARRIAGE?

I think this loss and all the grief is affecting my marriage.

Things feel distant and even strained at times.

We tend to fight more.

We don't even talk that much anymore.

I'm feeling more alone with each passing day.

What do I do with this?

When we get hit with a close, personal loss, our lives are upended. Everything goes topsy-turvy. We're impacted emotionally, mentally, physically, and spiritually. Our relationships change, and that includes our marriage or similar committed relationship.

All of us grieve differently. Even if our spouse or partner has suffered the same loss (like a child, for instance), our responses will vary. Our grief processes will not be the same. We're on the same grief road, but how we travel it might be vastly different.

Loss is stressful. The grief process can whittle away at even the closest relationship. If we feel unsupported by our mate, the resulting loneliness can seem like yet another dagger to our heart.

The first thing to remember is that no marriage ever stays the same. All relationships are dynamic and always moving. Hopefully, we're growing closer, but this isn't always the case. There are times when we're not on the same page. Over time, a creeping separateness can invade.

Loss gives us an opportunity to grow together through the pain. This takes both parties. Couple growth requires both people being on board and ready to work. One alone can't do it.

Each spouse or partner needs to do what they can to listen, understand, and support the other. This begins with us. It's always our choice whether to meet our spouse where they are and love them as they are.

Learning to forgive and release offenses and misunderstandings quickly is crucial in committed relationships, especially when we're already squeezed by loss and grief. We can't control our partner's responses, but we can intentionally forgive to protect our own hearts from festering bitterness.

Sharing openly about what's happening inside us is key. How our mate responds is up to them and beyond our control. Hopefully, we'll be greeted by listening ears and a supportive heart. Whatever the case, it's important that we do what we can to grieve in healthy ways and involve our partner as they are willing.

Find ways to accept your mate where they are, as they are, in this process. Do what you can to be compassionate, loving, and supportive. Hopefully, they will do the same.

Affirmation:

Since loss affects all my relationships, it will certainly impact my marriage too. I'll focus on grieving in healthy ways and invite my spouse to join me as they can or want to.

Suggestions:

Loss will certainly affect your relationship with your spouse or partner. Here are a few tips to consider as you walk this difficult road:

- Set your mind to be real about what's going on inside you, as much as you can. If they're willing to listen and support you, they can be a major player in your grief journey.

- If both of you have endured the same loss, be mindful that you will each grieve differently. Give your partner permission to grieve in their own way.

- Continue to focus on grieving in healthy ways and taking good care of yourself. This is a great gift you can give to yourself and your partner.

- If you find yourself drifting further from each other during this time, consider seeking some expert guidance. Counseling or grief coaching can be a huge benefit. We all need outside help, perspective, and reassurance at times.

Marriage and other committed relationships take work, forgiveness, and lots of patience. Be patient with yourself and your partner. Remember that now is not forever. Things will change.

58

HOW DO I PARENT WELL WHILE GRIEVING?

**How do I parent my kids well
while all this is happening?**

**I can barely function myself, much less be
what and who my kids need right now.**

**I need to be strong for them, but I feel
so incredibly weak and vulnerable.**

**I'm exhausted and there's not
enough of me to go around.**

I don't know how to do this.

Parenting is one of the hardest tasks on the planet. Add a significant loss to our lives and parenting can seem almost impossible.

Our hearts have been hit. Our emotions are all over the place. Our mental capacity is being squeezed. We're fatigued almost all the time. Perhaps we're battling deep spiritual questions raised by our loss.

All this gets added on top of the long list of our regular responsibilities. We need time and space to grieve, but our kids need us. We feel the pressure to "be strong" for them. No matter what's happening with us personally, we want them to feel nurtured, loved, and secure.

Our kids also need us to be human. Parents are a child's first role models. Our kids learn how to do life by watching us. They mimic our words and actions. Even long after we're adults, we find ourselves saying and doing some of what our parents did. Parental influence is incredibly profound and powerful.

Our kids will struggle in life. They will face adversity and difficulty. They will encounter deep, painful losses. They learn how to handle such things from watching us. It's important that we are real with them about the pain and difficulty of life (appropriate to their age, of course).

In other words, our children need to know how to grieve. They can learn some of that from us. As we take our grief seriously and process it in healthy ways, our kids benefit - not just now, but for years to come. Walking this grief road honestly and openly is a wonderful gift we can give our children.

How openly do we grieve in front of our children? Like the rest of grief, this is an individual decision based on who we are and who our kids are. We need to be ourselves and act in a manner consistent with our relationship with each child. We can strive for honest, open communication with each child according to their age.

Love is not only about nurture, provision, and protection. Love is also about teaching and preparation for life. The family is the child's most immediate and intimate training ground. Childhood and our teen years serve as our personal Boot Camp for the battles of adulthood.

Modeling healthy grieving needs to be part of our parenting. We're giving them permission to grieve as we grieve. We're sending the message that it's okay to feel sad or hurt when something painful happens.

Families learning to grieve together is a messy, challenging process, but it's also necessary, healthy, and good.

Consider how you might be honest about your grief and model healthy grieving for your kids. Your efforts will be a gift that can serve them well in the years and decades ahead.

Affirmation:

I can love my children by being open and honest about my grief in ways that fit their age and our relationship. I'll do what I can to model healthy grieving for them.

Suggestions:

Here are a few tips for you if you're parenting while grieving:

- Consider having an honest conversation with your children (perhaps each child individually) about what you're going through. How can you be open with them in a way that is appropriate to their age?

- If your children are enduring the same loss (they too had a relationship with the person who died), you can share how you're feeling and then ask how they've been feeling. Depending on their age, you might have a time where you all draw a picture related to the person who died and then share with each other. Or perhaps everyone could write the person a short note or letter. How can you promote simple opportunities to share and grieve together?

- Good self-care is key to good parenting. You're modeling for your kids how to live and what's important. Love them by grieving in healthy ways, one day, one step, one moment at a time.

As a parent, give yourself a lot of grace and kindness while grieving. Give up trying to be the perfect parent and focus on being honest and loving.

59

HOW DO I DEAL WITH THE TERRIBLE LONELINESS I FEEL?

I feel so alone.

I guess I imagined all this would be different somehow.

I thought others would be more supportive and kinder.

I never dreamed it would be this hard.

I feel isolated.

How do I deal with the terrible loneliness I feel?

The loneliness of grief can be deep and painful. We're designed for relationship. We're meant for connection. Loneliness is a heartache that grieving hearts are familiar with.

Loneliness is a human condition. With all our technology and ways to stay constantly "connected" to others, research shows that we feel more isolated than ever. "Alone together" might be an accurate way to describe how many of us feel.

When a close loss occurs, a new type of loneliness begins to emerge. We had a one-of-a-kind relationship with a unique person who was special to us. Though every human heart knows loss, this loss is unique to us. This loss is our own.

No one around us knows our hearts fully or truly how we feel. We don't even know the depths of our own hearts. Though the grief road is well populated, our grief journey can be incredibly lonely.

Feeling lonely in the grief process is natural, common, and to be expected.

This grief loneliness is in many ways healthy. It's consistent with reality. We're separated from someone we love and care about. We feel this separation. There is a new void in our lives. Our loneliness expresses our love and our longing.

We need supportive people who will share our loneliness. People can't take our loneliness away, but they can enter it with us. They can enter our world and walk with us in our grief for a little while. Healthy, safe people can make a huge difference in helping us move through this barren, lonely wasteland.

We need to remember the truth that things will change. As we move through the grief process in healthy ways, our grief loneliness will change over time. What that looks like is as individual as we are.

If you're feeling lonely in your grief, take a deep breath and look around you. Almost everyone is feeling lonely on some level. Though you feel lonely, you are not alone.

Affirmation:

I'll accept loneliness as a natural part of grief. I'll connect with safe people who can share my loneliness and walk with me on this journey.

Suggestions:

When grief loneliness strikes, here are some tips to consider:

- Process the loneliness in healthy ways. Try using T.W.A. - talk it out, write it out, art it out (see the end of chapter 10 for more information). Expressing what's happening inside you is key to healing, adjustment, recovery, and growth.

- Do your best to accept this loneliness as part of the grief journey. Tell yourself, "I feel lonely. That's okay. I'm missing someone. This is natural." Once our hearts accept that our loneliness is okay, natural, and to be expected, we can begin to relax a little. Nothing strange or weird is happening. We're feeling a new hole in our hearts.

- Connect with safe people who can share your loneliness. You need to be able to express what's happening inside to someone who will listen and love you where you are. When you feel seen and heard, you feel loved.

- Think about the people around you. Observe them. See if you can begin to sense the loneliness behind their smiles and laughter. Let a new sense of others' loneliness lead you to greater kindness and compassion. Even while grieving, your smile and authentic greeting can make a huge difference. You can be a comforter today, just by being present to those around you.

The grief road is lonely. Do what you can to accept yourself as you are and to process your loneliness in healthy ways.

60

DO SUPPORT GROUPS REALLY HELP?

I feel alone and misunderstood.

**People who said they would be
there for me have vanished.**

**Surely someone else out there is grieving
and understands what I'm going through.**

**I've heard of grief support groups,
but do they really help?**

I feel vulnerable and shaky.

I can't afford to be hurt any more right now.

We've been wounded deeply. We're missing someone special. Others losses have piled in on top of the death of our loved one or friend. We can feel overloaded and overwhelmed.

If we've been hurt in relationships, the thought of reaching out to others might be unnerving. We don't want any more pain. We might begin to cocoon. We withdraw and tell ourselves that our grief must be kept private. We hide and try to manage our loss and all the changes on our own.

We know support groups are out there, but we're reluctant to check them out. Getting together with people we don't know sounds artificial and risky. We've heard that such groups are beneficial to many, but we're skeptical about whether they would be helpful to us.

Finding and being with others who are grieving can be comforting and reassuring. Other wounded hearts are sympathetic and even empathetic. Loss has taught them compassion and acceptance.

Many times, we can find some of the safe people we need in support groups. Good facilitators can direct the sharing in a way that ends up being supportive and helpful to those present. Group ground rules often include things like confidentiality, acceptance of each participant as they are, and no giving of advice that hasn't been asked for.

The goal of a good support group is to provide a safe place where grieving hearts can be seen and heard.

Grief support groups are as different as the people in them. No two groups are the same. Some groups have no specific content or agenda. They simply exist for people to come together and support one another. Other groups have some content along with plenty of time for personal sharing. Still others might be heavy on content and light on personal stories and sharing.

Support groups can be refreshing and even restore some of our hope in other people. We can find new traveling companions for this painful, difficult journey. Connections built in these groups can become deep and lasting.

Are support groups for everyone? No, probably not. Yet we all need safe people in our lives, especially now. Even if we don't like the group as a whole, it's quite possible we could find a safe person to relate to and connect with.

If you haven't already, consider checking out a group in your area. There are virtual grief support groups as well. Though trying a group out might feel risky, the benefits could be massive.

Affirmation:

Support groups are helpful to many. I'll consider checking some out. Perhaps I'll find some of the safe people I need there.

Suggestions:

Support groups have been extremely helpful to many on the grief journey. If you're willing to consider a support group, here are some suggestions:

- Check with local hospices, churches, religious organizations, and civic groups. Many of these either have grief support groups or know about them. There are also many virtual support groups available online for those who prefer this or live in an area where no in-person groups are available.

- If just showing up feels scary, consider contacting the group facilitator, who can share more about the group and what they do. You could also ask a friend you trust to go with you to the first meeting.

- When you try a group, consider attending at least a couple of times before deciding whether it's for you. Each meeting is different, however, and all groups have some meetings that are "better" than others.

- If one group doesn't work out, please consider trying another. Finding the right group can be a bit like buying a new pair of shoes. Sometimes you must try on several to find one that fits.

Trying a support group can feel risky, but it can be well worth it.

61

WOULD COUNSELING HELP ME?

**I have bad days and better days, but all
of them are weighed down with grief.**

I feel like a phantom roaming about in a new world.

I'm hurting, but most people don't seem to care.

**Everyone just wants me to get
over it and stop grieving.**

I find myself wondering who I am now.

Would counseling help me?

"Would counseling help me?"

Many of us have asked this question.

If we have sought counseling before and had a positive experience, we're more likely to see the benefit and seek help.

If we have some sort of stigma about counseling, or are around others who do, we might be reluctant. Seeking professional assistance seems like an admission of personal weakness.

Most people are somewhere in between.

There are many times in life when we can use the listening ear and input of a trained professional. We do this with education, finances, house repairs, cars, etc. In grief, our hearts are at stake. That's huge. All of us could benefit from the acceptance and guidance of someone who knows the grieving heart well.

For some, the financial cost of counseling can be intimidating. Thankfully, many insurance plans have some counseling benefits. Those who benefit most from counseling see it as an investment in their hearts, health, healing, and relationships. It's an investment that can pay big dividends for the rest of their lives.

If we're isolating or having trouble functioning on a daily basis, counseling can help steady and strengthen us for this journey. If we're struggling deeply, reaching out for expert assistance is wise.

Who the counselor is matters. We need to feel safe, heard, and seen. Feeling like this is a "good fit" helps put us at ease and sets us up for healing and growth.

Professional counselors, grief therapists, grief coaches, and other grief professionals can play an important role in your grief process. Their acceptance, support, and perspective can make a huge difference.

Affirmation:

Many grieving hearts benefit from expert help. I'll consider whether counseling or grief coaching might be helpful on my grief journey.

Suggestions:

If you're wondering whether counseling or grief coaching might be beneficial for you, here are a few tips that might help:

- Check with local hospices, grief centers, or churches /faith centers about their grief support. They either have grief professionals on their staff, or they can direct you to counselors or grief coaches in your area.

- Many counselors and grief coaches offer virtual services via phone, Zoom, or other means. Though not physically in the same room, this option can be preferable to many for a variety of reasons. Many grief coaches, for example, offer a short, free consultation to see if they are a good fit for you.

- Ask around to see if anyone knows any grief professionals in your area. A personal recommendation from someone we know can be terrifically helpful and relieving.

- Sometimes, we just need to take the plunge. Consider trying a grief coaching or counseling session. Many of the best things in life are hard and scary at first.

If you're interested in knowing more about grief coaching, you can visit this page: **https://www.garyroe. com/coaching**

62

HOW DO I DEAL WITH UNSUPPORTIVE FAMILY?

I thought at least my family would be supportive.

I was wrong.

**A few tried to be sympathetic,
but that didn't last long.**

**They've judged me, tried to fix me,
and now are avoiding me.**

**To be fair, I don't want to be
around them much either.**

How do I deal with this?

When trouble comes, we naturally rely on those closest to us for support. If we get evaluated, judged, and belittled instead, the shock and pain only add to our grief.

Some have extremely supportive families. Others have no real family support of any kind. Most of us have something somewhere in-between - we have some relatives who are supportive and some who aren't.

Like friends and coworkers, most family members are sympathetic at first. As time wears on, some don't want to be reminded of the loss or have to deal with someone who is grieving. Some are so uncomfortable with emotional pain that they tend to swat at it like some pesky fly.

This general relational principle for the grief journey applies to family members too. Get around those who are helpful to you and limit your exposure to those who aren't. If you must be around unsupportive family members, do your best to guard your heart.

It would be nice if every member of our family was kind, compassionate, and supportive. We want it to be so. Of course, wishing doesn't make it reality. People are who they are. We all respond differently based on our own issues and our current mindset and situation.

Just as we want family members to allow us to grieve and let us be who we are right now, we can return the favor by letting them be who they are in the moment. We stop expecting them to get it. We downgrade our expectations. We're careful about sharing our grief around them because such expressions have not been welcomed or respected in the past.

We can't change our families or educate them into being compassionate and supportive. We can, however, search diligently for safety and support elsewhere. Safe people are out there, and they are ready and willing to walk with us.

There are many things we can't change. We can always choose, however, to do things that are healthy and healing. We focus on what we **can** do and try to release what we can't.

If your family has been a disappointment since your loss, you're not alone. This is a common phenomenon in the grief process. Focus on accepting what is, including your family as they are, and free yourself to pursue acceptance and support elsewhere.

Affirmation:

When my family is unsupportive, I'll accept things as they are rather than trying to change them. I'll seek the support I need elsewhere.

Suggestions:

If you have family members who are unsupportive, below are a few things to consider:

- Give your family permission to not understand and to not support you in ways that are helpful. Unmet expectations produce disappointment and can lead to ongoing frustration and anger.

- Release offenses. Forgive family members for what they have said and done and what they failed to say and do. Forgiveness says, "I release you from blame because I don't want what you have done and said to overly influence or rule my life." Forgiveness is a huge part of taking good care of yourself on this grief journey. Please see the end of chapter 52 for a helpful forgiveness exercise.

- If your family relationships allow this, consider sharing specifics about what's helpful to you right now and what's not. Calmly tell them what you need and let them tell you if they are willing to do that.

- Seek some safe people who can support you well during this time. We all desperately need people who know grief and who will accept us where we are. Be intentional about regularly connecting with safe people. For more information on safe people, see chapter 55.

- You can help yourself recover from a lack of family support by becoming supportive to those around you. Pay attention to those you encounter. Develop the habit of seeing and hearing them. You can be compassionate and supportive, even when others are not. This helps heal your heart.

Family relationships are often challenging. Grief can make them even more so.

"When our days become dreary with low-hovering clouds of despair, and when our nights become darker than a thousand midnights, let us remember that there is a creative force in this universe, working to pull down the gigantic mountains of evil, a power that is able to make a way out of no way and transform dark yesterdays into bright tomorrows."

—Martin Luther King Jr.

PART SIX:

THE FUTURE CHANGES

"My future is now a mystery.
I can no longer see ahead.
Everything has changed."
-Larry

63

WILL THIS EVER GET ANY BETTER?

Loss seems to have taken over my life.

I'm tired of pain and grief.

Will this ever get any better? If so, how? When?

How long is this going to go on?

Will things ever change?

Sometimes it feels like grief is my new life.

After a while, we can begin wondering what life will look like in the future. Our grief can be so intense, heavy, and all-consuming that we might wonder how long this is going to continue.

Will we ever feel any better? Will we heal? What does healing look like? Will we ever be the same again?

Will the grief ever end?

We're never the same after a loss. People are important. Life is about people and relationships. We attach and love. When someone dies, our hearts writhe. We now have a hole in our hearts. We will never be the same.

We will not go back to who we were before. That's impossible. As we process what's happening inside us, however, our grief will change over time. As we heal, the loss begins to settle into our minds and hearts. The original upheaval and emotional intensity will give way to a sort of continual ache.

Along the way, we will most likely continue to experience powerful grief bursts. These can come suddenly and seemingly out of nowhere. It can feel like the loss is happening all over again. These intense grief spikes are natural and common.

Everyone's journey is unique. The goal is to walk this road one day, one moment, one step at a time. As we make healthy choices and grieve well, healing takes place - whether we're aware of it or not. Over time, the "grief work" pays off and our hearts begin to adjust to the physical absence of someone special.

How long will we grieve? For as long as we miss them. In other words, when we think of our loved one or friend, experiencing some form of grief will always be natural and healthy. We will always love them, though we might not think of them as often as we once did.

If you're wondering if your grief will ever end, please know that this is a natural and common thought among grieving hearts. Loss is exhausting. Taking care of yourself is paramount. Keep expressing your grief in healthy ways.

Breathe deeply. Be patient with yourself, with others, and with the grief process. You can't hurry grief or push things along. This road can only be walked one step at a time.

Affirmation:

Rather than being consumed with feeling better, I'll focus on grieving well, one day, one step at a time. I'll trust that my grief will change as I heal, adjust, and recover.

Suggestions:

The length and intensity of the grief process can be grinding. No wonder we want to feel better and get some relief. Here are a few things to remind yourself of:

- You will never be the same, but you will heal, adjust, and grow through all this as you grieve in healthy ways.

- You may always grieve on some level because you will always miss them. As life reminds you of your loss, you will naturally grieve, but the grief will be different over time.

- Change is a huge constant in our lives. Your grief will change too.

- Grief cannot be forced or hurried. The grief process is not a checklist to be accomplished. Let the grief come as it wants to. Proactively express your grief in healthy ways by using T.W.A. (talk it out, write it out, art it out), connecting with safe people, and taking good care of yourself. See the end of chapter 10 for a detailed explanation of T.W.A.

- Grief bursts are natural and common. They can occur at any time. When these grief spikes come, breathe deeply and remind yourself that your heart is expressing itself. See chapter 16 for an explanation of how to handle these grief attacks.

You will always miss the one you lost. Honor them by expressing what's happening inside you honestly and as thoroughly as possible.

64

WHO AM I NOW?

I thought I knew who I was and what I was about.

Now, I'm not so sure.

So much has changed, including me.

I don't feel like myself anymore.

Have I lost myself too?

Who am I now?

Loss can throw us into an identity crisis.

Our worlds have been turned upside down. Someone special is missing. Our emotions are erratic and unpredictable. The pain inside can be intense. Our relationships are different. We don't feel like ourselves.

It's like a huge sinkhole opened up beneath us and we're in a free fall to who knows where. We might have had other losses, but we've never been here before. We've known other griefs, but this loss is unique.

When everything seems to have changed, it's natural to feel unsettled and shaky. We wonder what life will be like. We wonder who we are now and who we'll become.

In addition to losing a special someone, we can feel like we've lost ourselves too.

The truth is that we are **not** the same people we were. Our life has been altered, and we're changing to deal with this huge shift. Some sense of identity crisis during this season of grief is common for grieving hearts.

When we lose someone, we lose much of what was attached to them too - our routines, expectations, hopes, dreams, etc. The sheer amount of change is stunning. We're forced to adjust to a plethora of alterations we didn't want or ask for.

As we focus on expressing what's happening inside us and grieve in healthy ways, we will heal and grow. Time does not heal all wounds, but healing and adjustment do take time.

Loss can, if we're willing, teach us to live with more meaning and purpose than ever before. We can discover more about ourselves and why we are here. We can further define what's really important. How we live life can be deeply enriched, even in the face of great loss. Loss can train us to live more from our hearts.

All this might seem impossible now. As you process your grief, however, most likely the color will return to life. The loss will settle in at a deeper level. The grief you experience will change. Your sense of your own identity may undergo some intense examination, but you can come through this even more compassionate, kind, and loving.

Let the grief come. Express it honestly and in healthy ways. Honor the one you're missing with how you live. As you heal, grow, and serve others, who you are now will become more and more clear.

Affirmation:

I'll remember that loss rattles my sense of who I am. I'll let the grief come, process it well, and trust that I'll grow into more of who I am through all this.

Suggestions:

If you're struggling with your sense of identity and wondering who you are now, here are some tips you might find helpful:

- Remember that your sense of who you are is always in process. We discover more of who we are through life, experiences, relationships, and losses. Like gold is refined through fire, your identity and character are molded by difficulties, trials, and losses.

- Let your grief become fuel for service. This honors your loved one. Living well is about kindness, compassion, and love.

Consider using T.W.A. to process this issue of personal identity.

- How do you see yourself as different because of this loss?

- Are there parts of yourself you feel like you've lost?

- How do you sense you have grown through this loss so far?

- Who would you like to be on the back side of all this?

- Are there ways you can see yourself using your grief as fuel to serve others?

Much of life is about overcoming. Don't let loss define who you are, but rather find ways to use what happens for good somehow.

65

HOW AND WHEN SHOULD I DEAL WITH MY LOVED ONE'S POSSESSIONS?

I'm surrounded by memories and reminders.

My loved one's belongings are everywhere.

I get shaky every time I think about doing something with them.

Perhaps I should leave everything as is.

How and when should I deal with their possessions?

Our loved one's belongings are a constant reminder of what was but is no more. Their possessions become the physical representation of them to us. Each object or piece of clothing can be packed with meaning and memories.

For some, the thought of doing anything with their loved one's belongings is terrifying. These objects can become sacred to us. Putting them away becomes synonymous with rejecting our loved one somehow.

For others, being surrounded by these reminders is too painful. Almost on impulse, we find ourselves dealing quickly with their belongings. Sometimes the situation itself necessitates that we do this.

Since every grief process is unique, there is no one right way to approach this dilemma. The goal for all of us is to grieve in healthy ways, and how we manage our loved one's possessions is a part of that. We want to find a path that allows us to grieve well and honors our relationship with the one we've lost.

For most, the answer lies inside our hearts. What seems natural and good to us? What seems to fit with who we are and our grief?

Do we deal with their belongings all at once, or a little at a time? How and where do we begin? When?

For most grieving hearts, it's hard to know all the answers at one time. We tend to discover what to do and when as we take the next step, whatever that is. This grief walk can only be taken one step at a time.

We often create extra burdens for ourselves by trying to look too far ahead and figure everything out. This comes from our desire to have some control at a time when things feel uncertain and foggy. We do better when we release our expectations of what should happen and when, and then simply focus on the next step.

Tussling with how to handle our loved one's things is natural and common for grieving hearts. It can be an intense, heavy, and difficult process. Being kind to yourself and patient with yourself is important. Give your heart the time and space it needs.

When you're ready, take just the first step. As you do, the next step will become apparent in its time.

Affirmation:

**When it comes to my loved one's posses-
sions, I'll pay attention to my heart. I'll take
one step at a time and trust the next step
will become apparent in its own time.**

Suggestions:

Here are some tips for facing the highly emotional task of
dealing with your loved one's belongings:

- Consider processing this a bit before diving in. Perhaps use T.W.A. (talk it out, write it out, art it out)
  to express what you're thinking and feeling about
  this. You might be surprised at what you discover.
  Processing some of this beforehand can help greatly
  in knowing what to do and when.

- Pay attention to your heart. What do you sense is
  the next step? Consider taking this next step while
  trying not to look too far ahead.

- As you deal with their things, pay attention to what's
  happening inside you. Take your time and process
  your thoughts and emotions as you go. What are
  you feeling? What are the thoughts behind those
  emotions? Handling their belongings is a natural opportunity to express the grief inside you. "Get it out"
  as best you can.

- Be ready for all this to occur in phases over time.
  Like the rest of grief, dealing with your loved one's
  possessions is a process and will most likely take
  time.

Let self-care be your priority in all this. Taking good care of yourself honors your loved one.

66

HOW DO I MAKE GOOD DECISIONS WHILE GRIEVING?

There are so many decisions to be made.

I'm on overload.

Sometimes, I can't seem to make any decisions at all.

It's like I'm paralyzed.

How do I make good decisions while grieving?

Decision-making can be a huge challenge for grieving hearts.

For some, the sheer number of decisions that must be made after a death can be staggering. Like a sudden avalanche, we can find ourselves swept along in the current of what the world and everyone else tells us needs to be done and when.

Some decisions must be made in a certain timeframe. We breathe deeply and do our best with these things. Hopefully, a few safe people around us are assisting in this. It's not about making the perfect choice, because it's impossible to know what that would be. We simply try to live from our hearts in that moment as much as we can.

We can only work with what we have in any given moment. When squeezed by heavy grief, there's less of us available to make some of these urgent decisions. We seek the help of those we trust and give ourselves the grace we need in the moment.

Of course, all decisions are not the same when it comes to their level of importance.

Some decisions are minor, while others are life-altering. In previous chapters, we've talked about how our mental capabilities are impacted by loss. We're not at our best right now. We don't see things as clearly. Making small decisions is part of our daily routine. Making large decisions, however, is not wise during a season of heavy grief.

Not all big decisions can be put off, however. With the help of some safe people, you can determine which decisions need to be made and which ones are better tabled for a while. Most of us have enough regrets already. We don't want to add more through hasty decision-making during this confusing time.

When emotions are high, our decision-making tends to turn impulsive. As humans, when life gets painful, we naturally go into fight-or-flight mode. We either act or shut down. Neither option is optimal. Many find that resisting the temptation to make the big decision now gives them time to make the better decision later.

In the grief world it's often advised, "No major, life-altering decisions in the first six months to a year after a loss." Many who have been through heavy grief can attest to the truth of this. As we give ourselves time and space to grieve and process what's happening inside us, decision making tends to become clearer over time.

Take your time with important decisions. What's not clear now might become so later. Focus on grieving well.

Affirmation:

If possible, I'll avoid making life-altering decisions at times of heavy grief. I'll be patient and trust that I'll get the clarity and guidance I need as I process my grief well.

Suggestions:

When it comes to decision-making in grief, here are some guidelines you might find helpful:

- If the decision is minor and needs to be made quickly, simply make the best choice you can. Trust your heart. If you're in doubt, reach out to someone you trust for input.

- If the decision you're facing is a major one, ask yourself if this can be put off for a while. If a decision must be made quickly, consult others you trust who have your best interests in mind.

- Pay attention to your heart. Do what you can to process and express the emotions and thoughts you experience as you encounter decisions. The more you process what's happening inside as you go, the clearer things will most likely become down the road.

- Make self-care your priority. As you take care of yourself first, many decisions will become easier to make. If you allow the pressure of the decisions to set the agenda, it's easy to get frustrated, confused, and angry. For more on self-care, see chapter 39.

Decision-making while grieving is tough. Unless the issue is urgent, take your time.

67

HOW DO I THINK ABOUT THE FUTURE NOW?

**I didn't know it at the time, but my
future died with my loved one.**

**Many of the expectations, hopes, and
dreams I had are now gone.**

The future has been altered.

I don't know what to do with this.

How do I think about the future now?

When someone close to us dies, our lives change. We're not aware of it at the time, but our future was significantly altered the moment their heart stopped beating.

As we move through our grief process, we're met with more losses along the way. Everything in our lives attached to our loved one or friend has been affected or even lost. Many of the things we anticipated are no longer possible. Some hopes and dreams died along with them.

We look ahead and don't recognize the landscape. The future has become unclear and hazy. For some of us, the road ahead might seem to have disappeared entirely.

How do we deal with this?

The first key is to accept what is. This includes accepting ourselves as we are in the moment, with all our wonderings, concerns, and fears.

Second, it's good to recognize the truth that none of us ever knows the specifics of what's down the road. We don't know what today will bring, much less the next month, year, or decade. We plan. We build expectations, hopes, and dreams. And yet, we know things will probably not turn out exactly like we envisioned. We are not in control. Life and loss interrupt our finely laid plans.

The future is uncharted territory. It always has been.

Third, as we continue to process our grief in healthy ways, the road ahead becomes a little more visible over time. We focus on living as much as possible in the present moment. We take one moment, one day at a time. We take the next step while trying not to look too far ahead. Step by step, we inch into the future and learn moment by moment how to live amid this new reality we find ourselves in.

It can be hard to make long-range plans while grieving. Taking care of ourselves and processing this loss well gobbles up most of our routine. If we're willing, loss can teach us to live life as it should be lived - in the now, one moment, one step at a time.

Affirmation:

It's okay if my future appears hazy and uncertain. I'll see things more clearly as I move through my grief, one step at a time.

Suggestions:

If it feels like your future has been upended, you are not alone. Many grieving hearts experience this. Here are some tips for when the road ahead is hazy:

- Consider using T.W.A. (talk it out, write it out, art it out) to process your thoughts and feelings about the future. What do you find yourself wondering about? What are your worries, concerns, and fears? Expressing what's happening inside you and "getting it out" is essential. See the end of chapter 10 for more information on T.W.A.

- Connect with others who know grief. Share with them what you're thinking and feeling. Ask them about how they view the future. This can help bring perspective. It will also reassure us that we're normal and not crazy. The sense of comradery with those who "get it" can be profoundly comforting.

- If you haven't already, consider trying a support group. Others who are grieving can often go beyond sympathy to empathy. Many of them will have the same concerns you do about the future. For more on support groups, see chapter 58.

Remember that now is not forever. As you work through your grief, your view of your future will change. Just because the future seems foggy now doesn't mean it can't be good.

68

HOW DO I HANDLE SPECIAL DAYS?

**One of those special days is coming
up, and I don't know what to do.**

I'm dreading it.

I want to hide.

**Yet, I know the day will come
anyway, no matter what.**

How do I survive this?

Our calendars are full of special days. Holidays. Birthdays. Anniversaries. Thanksgiving. Christmas. The list goes on and on.

And now we have another "special day" to consider - the death anniversary of the one we lost.

For grieving hearts, these special times on the calendar are anxiety-producing, frustrating, and painful. Our hearts sense when one of these days is approaching, even if our minds haven't actually thought of it yet. We're designed for connection. We're still attached, even though our loved one or friend is no longer here.

Special days and holidays surface our losses like nothing else can. We seem to bump into a memory with every step. Everything reminds us of our loss. Facing these days can feel like a solo climb of Mount Everest.

For most of us, our first instinct is to hide, hunker down, and wait for this storm to pass. This is indeed an option, but it doesn't help us much on our grief journey. In fact, trying to run from these days only sets us up for more pain and anxiety down the road.

So, what can we do?

We can shift our mindset to using these days in positive ways to help us grieve. We can make a simple plan to intentionally remember our friend or loved one and honor them somehow.

We might light a candle in their honor or donate to a charity in their name. We could serve in a cause that was important to them. We might write them a letter or express our gratitude for them in a journal. We could even invite a few people to join us that day and have a time of memory sharing. There are many options.

As we proactively plan for the coming special day, chances are part of our dread will be released. As we move through the day remembering and honoring them, we give ourselves an important opportunity to express what we're feeling and thinking. The day will likely be emotional and even painful, but it can still be good.

As special days come, focus on using them rather than letting them use you. Set your sights on grieving in healthy ways by making a simple plan to remember and honor the one you've lost.

Affirmation:

As special days approach, I'll make a simple plan to remember and honor my loved one. This honors both of us and our relationship.

Suggestions:

If you find yourself dreading special days, please know that almost all grieving hearts tussle with this. You are far from alone. Here are some things you can do to navigate these pain points on the calendar:

- Make a simple plan for the next special day on the calendar. What are your concerns and worries? What special memories do you have of this day? What might you do to intentionally remember and honor your friend or loved one on this day?

- Connect with others who know grief well. Many have been through numerous special days on their grief journey. Share with them about your upcoming special day. Listen to their wisdom. They will assure you that what you're feeling is normal and common.

- If you're in a support group, share about this upcoming day with them. The group may have helpful insights. Together, you can help each other meet the special days ahead. For more info on support groups, see chapter 60.

- When the special day comes, be prepared for grief bursts. There may be many grief triggers during the day. That's natural and to be expected. It will be an emotional day, but you can use it for good - to help you grieve and to honor your loved one.

- If you can, try to include others in your plan for this special day. This gives others a chance to share and to grieve. This helps everyone.

Special days are hard. Make a simple plan to use these days to take good care of yourself and to honor your loved one.

69

HOW CAN I USE MY GRIEF FOR GOOD?

I don't want to mope about and have pity parties.

I want to honor my loved one.

**I want to move through this grief,
heal, and make a difference.**

I need to use all this for good somehow.

How can I make all this pain and grief count?

———————

When our grief is intense, we can feel hijacked. Loss has taken over our lives. The pain, confusion, and upset can rule our routine.

We want and need to grieve. We've lost someone special. We have a new hole in our hearts. Our hearts, minds, bodies, souls, relationships, and future are all impacted. The sheer weight of all the changes can be crushing.

And yet, we need meaning and purpose during this time. Finding ways to serve others, even while we're hurting, is part of the grief and healing process. For many grieving hearts, using their grief for the good of others brings comfort, perspective, and some peace amid this current storm.

It can be challenging to look outside ourselves at a time when we want to draw inward. Putting ourselves out there for others when our personal energy tank is almost empty might seem strange or even foolish. Even so, many find that intentionally focusing on others gets them out of their own head and brings some much-needed grief relief.

Serving others brings a unique joy to the heart and soul. When we engage in loving others, it feels good and right. Meeting people in their worlds and accepting them as they are (doing for them what we wish others would do for us) is a tremendous gift both to them and to ourselves. Many times, we end up receiving by giving.

How can we serve others during this time? How can we make this grief and pain count?

We might volunteer and meet an important need in a cause or organization we're passionate about.

If we're in a support group, we could talk to the facilitator about how we might serve other members.

We could be a safe person for someone else who's grieving and support them in their journey.

We might simply think about the people immediately around us and ask ourselves how we might express kindness to them. Small acts of kindness - a greeting, a smile, a small gift, an encouraging note, etc. - are far more powerful than any of us realize.

Your heart hungers for meaning and purpose, especially in times of loss. How can you use your grief for good by serving others? Get creative. Keep it simple and realistic. Be bold. You are more important than you realize. You have more to give than you can imagine.

You can make a huge difference in the lives of others even while grieving. What a wonderful way to honor the one you've lost.

Affirmation:

I'll find ways to use my pain and grief for good. I'll engage in simple acts of kindness and serve others as part of my grief journey.

Suggestions:

We can make a difference in the world, even during seasons of heavy loss:

- Remind yourself that you have great meaning and purpose, even though your heart might be broken at present. Broken hearts can make a massive impact for good. Tell yourself, "I can use my grief for good. I can use this pain to make a difference."

- What simple acts of kindness can you engage in? How can you serve those immediately around you? Is there an organization or cause you would consider being involved in? Take some time and think through the options.

- Talk with the safe people in your life about how you might serve others. They might surprise you with some wonderful ideas that would never occur to you.

- At first, keep it simple. Be realistic about what you can do and how much. Better to start small and build over time rather than attempting something large and burning out.

You don't have to be at your best to express kindness and serve others. You'll be surprised at the positive impact you can have even while grieving.

70

HOW DO I MOVE FORWARD WITHOUT LEAVING MY LOVED ONE BEHIND?

I want to live well.

I know my loved one would want this.

People keep telling me I have to say good-bye, but I don't know what that means.

I don't want to say goodbye.

Honestly, I'm afraid of moving forward.

I can't stand the thought of leaving my loved one behind somehow.

Many grieving hearts are reticent about the words "moving forward." It sounds as if our loved one is stuck in the past. If we want to be with them, we naturally think we must live in the past. The world is plowing forward as usual, but our personal timeline stopped at the time of their death.

If moving forward has to do with somehow leaving our loved one or friend behind or having them less present in our hearts, we don't want anything to do with it. We loved them, and we love them still. We miss them. We don't like this separation or this new life we find ourselves living.

Naturally, our hearts want to take them with us somehow. The good news is that we can do just that.

Even though their physical presence is gone, their influence resides in us. They speak to us through their past words and actions. All we received from them is now a part of us. They have a forever place in our hearts.

In many ways, we take them with us wherever we go. As we "move forward," we don't leave them behind. We move on with them, but in new and different ways.

We say goodbye to their physical presence - their touch, their companionship, and their former role in our routines. We do not say goodbye, however, to their powerful influence in our lives, both now and in the future.

Perhaps we'll ask, "What would they do in this situation?" We smile at things they would smile at and grieve at situations that would cause them pain. Their wisdom and insight come to us at important times of decision-making. They are with us in so many ways.

Your loved one's or friend's physical presence is gone, but they are still with you - and will be - in many ways. Let this reality bring a deep sense of gratitude for all that they were and are to you.

We are truly relational creatures. We attach and love. Love endures.

Affirmation:

Though I miss their physical presence, my loved one's influence will never fade. I get to take them forward with me in many ways.

Suggestions:

Here are a few tips to help you process this chapter:

- Tell yourself the truth. "My loved one has died and is no longer physically with me. Their words, actions, and influence remain with me always."

- Consider brainstorming the ways your loved one is still with you. Think of their words, actions, and influence in your life. Make a list of what comes to mind. Afterwards, read through this list. Express thanks for their incredible role in your life.

- Talk with your safe person or support group about this. See what they think. Consider sharing with each other how those who have died still have great influence on your lives today.

- What would you say is your loved one's or friend's greatest legacy to you? Think in terms of character, not possessions. Are there ways you can further honor them by living their legacy?

You take the one you lost with you, in many ways. Their influence remains.

71

HOW CAN I HELP OTHERS
WHO ARE GRIEVING?

Now that I have experienced this terrible pain, I am more compassionate.

In the past, I judged others who were grieving.

I had no idea what they were going through.

Now, I know.

I want to make a difference.

How can I help others who are grieving?

Before we knew loss, perhaps we were insensitive to those around us who were grieving. We weren't aware of what they were going through. We didn't know.

Now that we know the terrible pain of losing someone special, we can be more compassionate. We can allow this loss to teach us to live with more kindness and love than ever before. This honors the one we lost and is a great gift to ourselves and others.

If we want to care effectively for others who are grieving, we need to set our sights on becoming safe people.

We want to become people who have no agenda for others except to meet them where they are, accept them as they are, and walk with them in their world.

To support others, we focus on being as present as possible and listening without judgment. Our goal becomes to see and hear the hearts of those around us.

We let them vent. We sit with them while they express their grief and pain. We listen attentively to their thoughts and feelings. We let them "get it out." We focus on them and not on how we're going to respond.

We don't try to help them feel better. We don't try to fix anything. We don't give them advice they haven't asked for. We do our best not to read ourselves into what they're saying. We resist making it about us.

We know from our own experience that we heal, adjust, and recover as we express our grief in healthy ways and feel seen and heard by a few safe people. We now give that gift to others. We don't have to "do" anything except show up in their lives and be with them in their world.

We can care for other grieving hearts in many ways. Acts of kindness and service. Warm gestures of acceptance and support through messages, letters, cards, emails, or even texts. Our task is not to be everything to them, but rather to be who we are and support them as we can along the way.

You can make a big difference in the lives of others now that you know the pain of close loss. You can be kind and compassionate in ways others cannot. You can be part of the comforting salve their wounded hearts need along this bumpy, difficult journey.

We all need good traveling companions for this grief road.

Affirmation:

I will use the pain of this loss for good.
I will seek to become a safe person
for others who are grieving.

Suggestions:

If you desire to become a safe person who can support others who are grieving, here are a few tips for you:

- Don't expect yourself to get this right or perfect. None of us are 100% safe all the time. We make mistakes. Give yourself lots of grace and room to grow in learning to support others well.

- Practice listening. Practice being quiet while other people share with you. Focus on them. Try to not to evaluate or judge anything. Just listen.

- As you listen, try to hear past their words and glimpse a little of their heart. Allow yourself to sense some of their pain, confusion, sadness, and frustration.

- As you listen, your own grief might get triggered. This is natural. If you can, set that aside for now. When you're alone, come back to this point in your mind and begin to process what happened. Supporting others who are grieving will give you a unique opportunity to further process your own grief and pain.

As you process your own grief, you can make a huge difference in the lives of others, especially those who are grieving.

CONCLUDING THOUGHTS

There's no doubt about it. Loss is painful. The grief journey is difficult. We've covered a lot together in this book. In summary, all these questions, answers, and suggestions boil down to a few keys:

Remember that life is not business as usual. Your world has changed.

Be kind to yourself and patient with yourself. This is hard and exhausting.

Do what you can to process your grief and "get it out" by expressing it in healthy ways.

Remind yourself that now is not forever. Things will change.

Do your best to accept yourself as you are in the moment.

Connect with people who are helpful to you and limit your exposure to those who aren't.

Find ways to use your grief for good. Serving others helps heal your broken heart.

This is a long, arduous road. Pace yourself well. Find good traveling companions. Take one day, one moment, one step at a time.

You're not alone, though many times it might feel that way.

You're not crazy, but you've been thrust into a crazy-making situation compared to your old routine.

You will make it through this, though sometimes you might wonder how.

I leave with you one of my favorite Bible passages:

"He will wipe every tear from their eyes. There will be no more death or mourning or crying or pain, for the old order of things has passed away." He who was seated on the throne said, "I am making everything new!" (Revelation 21:4-5)

———————————

Comfort, healing, and peace to you.

For more healing helps and resources,
visit **www.garyroe.com**.

ADDITIONAL GRIEF RESOURCES

THE COMFORT SERIES

www.garyroe.com/comfort-series

Comfort for Grieving Hearts: Hope and Encouragement in Times of Loss

Comfort for the Grieving Spouse's Heart: Hope and Healing After Losing Your Partner

Comfort for the Grieving Adult Child's Heart: Hope and Healing After Losing Your Parent

Comfort for the Grieving Parent's Heart: Hope and Healing After Losing Your Child

THE GOD AND GRIEF SERIES

https://www.garyroe.com/god-and-grief-series

Grief Walk: Experiencing God After the Loss of a Loved One

Widowed Walk: Experiencing God After the Loss of a Spouse

Orphaned Walk: Experiencing God After the Loss of a Parent

THE GOOD GRIEF SERIES

https://www.garyroe.com/good-grief-series/

Aftermath: Picking Up the Pieces After a Suicide
www.garyroe.com/aftermath

Shattered: Surviving the Loss of a Child
www.garyroe.com/shattered

Teen Grief: Caring for the Grieving Teenage Heart
www.garyroe.com/teengrief

Please Be Patient, I'm Grieving: How to Care for and Support the Grieving Heart
www.garyroe.com/please-be-patient

Heartbroken: Healing from the Loss of a Spouse
www.garyroe.com/heartbroken-2

Surviving the Holidays Without You: Navigating Loss During Special Seasons
www.garyroe.com/surviving-the-holidays

THE DIFFERENCE MAKER SERIES

www.garyroe.com/difference-maker

Difference Maker: Overcoming Adversity and Turning Pain into Purpose, Every Day (Adult & Teen Editions)

Living on the Edge: How to Fight and Win the Battle for Your Mind and Heart (Adult & Teen Editions)

FREE ON GARY'S WEBSITE

Grief: 9 Things I Wish I had Known

In this deeply personal and practical eBook, Gary shares nine key lessons from his own grief journeys. "This was so helpful! I saw myself on every page," said one reader. "I wish I had read this years ago," said another. Widely popular, this eBook has brought hope and comfort to thousands of grieving hearts.

Available at **www.garyroe.com.**

The Good Grief Mini-Course

Full of personal stories, inspirational content, and practical assignments, this 8-session email series is designed to help readers understand grief and deal with its roller-coaster emotions. Thousands have been through this course, which is now being used in support groups as well.

Available at **www.garyroe.com**.

The Hole in My Heart: Tackling Grief 's Tough Questions

This eBook tackles some of grief's big questions: "How did this happen?" "Why?" "Am I crazy?" "Am I normal?"

"Will this get any easier?" plus others. Written in the first person, it engages and comforts the heart.

Available at **www.garyroe.com**.

I Miss You: A Holiday Survival Kit

Thousands have downloaded this brief, easy-to-read, and very personal e-book. **I Miss You** provides some basic, simple tools on how to use holiday and special times to grieve well and love those around you.

Available at **www.garyroe.com**.

Help us reach other grieving hearts.

Share this link:

www.garyroe.com/grief-guidebook

CARING FOR GRIEVING HEARTS

Visit Gary at **www.garyroe.com** and connect with him on Facebook, Twitter, LinkedIn, and Pinterest.

Links:

Facebook: **https://www.facebook.com/garyroeauthor**

Twitter: **https://twitter.com/GaryRoeAuthor**

LinkedIn: **https://www.linkedin.com/in/garyroeauthor**

Pinterest: **https://www.pinterest.com/garyroe79/**

ABOUT THE AUTHOR

Gary's story began with a childhood of mixed messages and sexual abuse. This was followed by other losses and numerous grief experiences.

Ultimately, a painful past led Gary into a life of helping wounded people heal and grow. A former college minister, missionary in Japan, entrepreneur in Hawaii, and pastor in Texas and Washington, he now serves as a writer, speaker, chaplain, and grief counselor.

In addition to **The Grief Guidebook**, Gary is the author of numerous books, including the award-winning bestsellers **Shattered: Surviving the Loss of a Child**, **Comfort for the Grieving Spouse's Heart**, **Comfort for the Grieving Adult Child's Heart**, and **Aftermath: Picking Up the Pieces After a Suicide**. Gary's books have won four international book awards and have been named finalists seven times. He has been featured on Dr. Laura, Belief Net, the Christian Broadcasting Network, Wellness,

Thrive Global, and other major media and has well over 800 grief-related articles in print. Recipient of the Diane Duncam Award for Excellence in Hospice Care, Gary is a popular keynote, conference, and seminar speaker at a wide variety of venues.

Gary loves being a husband and father. He has seven adopted children, including three daughters from Colombia. He enjoys hockey, corny jokes, good puns, and colorful Hawaiian shirts. Gary and his wife Jen and family live in Texas.

Visit Gary at **www.garyroe.com**.

Don't forget to download your free eBook (PDF):

Grief: 9 Things I Wish I Had Known

**https://www.garyroe.com/
grief-9-things-i-wish-i-had-known-ebook/**

ACKNOWLEDGMENTS

Special thanks for my lovely wife Jen for her unwavering support and encouragement. Thank you for engaging with me in helping grieving hearts heal and grow.

Special thanks to Kathy Trim and Kelli Levey Reynolds for their keen proofreading eyes and editorial assistance. I appreciate you more than you know.

Thanks to my Advance Reader Team for helping make this book all it can be. You folks are amazing.

Thanks to Dr. Craig Borchardt of Hospice Brazos Valley for his continued support in producing quality resources for grieving hearts. It's an honor to know you.

Thanks to Glendon Haddix of Streetlight Graphics for his artistic skill and expertise in design and formatting. Your artistry continues to bring healing and hope to many.

AN URGENT PLEA

HELP OTHER GRIEVING HEARTS

Dear Reader,

Others are hurting and grieving today. You can help.

How?

With a simple, heartfelt review.

Could you take a few moments and write a 1-3 sentence review of **The Grief Guidebook: Common Questions, Compassionate Answers, Practical Suggestions** and leave it on the site you purchased the book from?

And if you want to help even more, you could leave the same review on **The Grief Guidebook** book page on Goodreads.

Your review counts and will help reach others who could benefit from this book.

Thanks for considering this. I read these reviews as well, and your comments and feedback assist me in producing more quality resources for grieving hearts.

Thank you!

Warmly,

Gary

Don't forget to download your free eBook (PDF):
Grief: 9 Things I Wish I Had Known
https://www.garyroe.com/
grief-9-things-i-wish-i-had-known-ebook/

Printed in Great Britain
by Amazon

11787351R00174